INTERNATIONAL TRADE - ON THE BRINK OF CHANGE

Edited by **Anita Maček**

International Trade - On the Brink of Change
http://dx.doi.org/10.5772/63143
Edited by Anita Maček

Contributors

Turkmen Goksel, Chan Tze-Haw, Susan Oliveira, Ntambwe Malangu, Rasto Ovin, Andrej Raspor, Ana Stranjančević, Iva Bulatović, Darko Lacmanović

Published by InTech

Janeza Trdine 9, 51000 Rijeka, Croatia

Publishing Process Manager Iva Lipovic

Technical Editor SPi Global

Cover InTech Design team

First published January, 2017

Printed in Croatia

Additional hard copies can be obtained from orders@intechopen.com

International Trade - On the Brink of Change, Edited by Anita Maček

p. cm.

Print ISBN 978-953-51-2911-0
Online ISBN 978-953-51-2912-7

For EU product safety concerns:
IN TECH d.o.o., Prolaz Marije Krucifikse Kozulić 3, 51000 Rijeka, Croatia,
info@intechopen.com or visit our website at intechopen.com.

Meet the editor

Anita Maček holds a PhD degree in Economics (2009) from the University of Maribor, Faculty of Economics and Business. She was the first in generation of doctoral students promoted by the National Technology Agency of Slovenia. In 2011, she was elected as an assistant professor—the youngest in the field of social science at the University of Maribor. Currently, she is employed at FH Joanneum, University of Applied Sciences, Graz, Austria, and at DOBA Faculty of Applied Business and Social Studies, Maribor, Slovenia. In 2016, she became an associate professor of Economics. Her main research interests are international capital flows, foreign direct investments, international business, smart cities and regional development.

Contents

Preface

Based on previous observations, there is no doubt that trade enhanced economic growth. This is especially valid in regard to international trade as it can help or hinder entire regions, thus adding to the issue of international security. Therefore, it is understandable that, especially following WW II, there have been numerous international arrangements put together with the goal of fostering international trade.

The General Agreement on Tariffs and Trade (GATT) was a multilateral agreement regulating international trade that took effect on January 1, 1948, and lasted until the signing of the Uruguay Round Agreements, which established the World Trade Organization (WTO) on January 1, 1995. The WTO, which deals with the rules of global trade between nations, has the main function of ensuring that trade flows as smoothly, predictably and freely as possible. On January 1, 1994, the North American Free Trade Agreement (NAFTA) came into effect, creating one of the world's largest free trade zones and laying the foundations for strong economic growth and rising prosperity for Canada, the USA and Mexico. Since then, NAFTA has demonstrated how free trade increases wealth and competitiveness, delivering real benefits to families, farmers, workers, manufacturers and consumers.

The European Union (EU) is a politico-economic union of 28 member states that are located primarily in Europe. The EU has developed an internal single market through a standardized system of laws that apply in all member states. EU policies aim to allow the free movement of people, goods, services and capital within the internal market; enact legislation in justice and home affairs and maintain common policies on trade, agriculture, fisheries and regional development.

Currently, trends are demonstrating how the path of globalization based on trade agreements is being questioned, and support for these agreements seems to have lost its momentum.

Opposition to free trade agreements and other international freedoms recently became the centrepiece of the campaigns of rising nationalist political parties, even in world's most developed economies. Their leaders usually claim that international trade agreements strip jobs out of national labour markets by moving production out of their economies. Here we see two basic problems. Such a position shows lack of basic and general knowledge regarding international trade benefits. Second, the current level of technology has, especially in business and politics, enabled global transparency of processes and actions. To withstand its development is not only a "policy of yesterday" but of the "day before yesterday". In the case of Brexit, one can even spot attempts to exclude regulations on free movement (people), yet retain other benefits of an internal market.

These facts raise a question: Are new threats to international co-operation and trade a demonstration of the backfiring of the globalization? Being often cited as a matter of Western interest and a tool for extracting profits from other regions, it caused a fall of traditional professions and industries that had employed millions of workers in the strongest world economies such as the USA and the UK.

In this book, we tried to collect texts that would not repeat known facts on international trade but would rather discuss special issues. Furthermore, we also wanted to bring regional perspectives. Therefore, this book is organized into two sections.

The section on "Selected Perspectives on International Trade" provides views which add to typical discussions on international trade. This section begins with a chapter that focuses on the implications of a decline in import costs to the welfare of the liberalizing country. The model numerically proves that unilateral trade liberalization is welfare improving for the liberalizing country in the Armington setup with iceberg trade costs. However, when using tariffs rather than iceberg trade costs, it is numerically shown that there exists a positive optimal tariff rate that maximizes welfare. This result indicates that a reduction in tariffs may either benefit or immiserize the liberalizing country depending on the pre-liberalization value of tariff.

The second chapter in this section looks at the discussion on fair trade initiatives and their possible role in achieving more equilibrated trade relations inside globalization and governance. The authors want to challenge the overrated goodwill of people's initiative mostly by positioning the said goodwill as a counterpart of existing trade policy developments. In this chapter, fair trade is passed through the principles of economics, which leads to a conclusion that the present concept is too narrow to produce enough inside energy for its establishment in a real policy of developed economies. They take the position that, due to its influence on domestic employment, fair trade is actually of strong interest of developed economies. The authors pay special attention to governance as a field that may profoundly explain the gaps subject to action in the fair trade initiatives. Due to the global meaning of the principle for sustainable global trade and security, it must continuously be more and more incorporated in the mainstream politics of world leading economies.

In the third chapter of this section, the authors highlight the risks associated with the trade of medicines by unlicensed organizations and non-professionals. These risks include the production and sale of counterfeit medicines, encouraging abuse and misuse of medicines, anti-competitive behaviour, etc. In this chapter, reasons and factors that sustain the trading of medicines by non-licensed businesses and non-professionals as well as the sources of medicines sold informally are discussed. The major findings are that the concessions made to allow non-licensed businesses and non-professionals to trade in medicines have resulted in several consequences that are threatening the whole world.

The section "Regional Specific Issues of International Trade" consists of three chapters. The first chapter in this section discusses the impacts of globalization on international trade patterns and the required shifts in trade policies. Highlighting the effects of production fragmentation, geographic dispersion and the expansion of global value chains, the chapter outlines the Brazilian experience to illustrate the difficulties that various countries face in acknowledging this economic reality and providing appropriate policy responses. Results of the analysis shown in the chapter have led to the conclusion that a non-GVC-oriented trade policy has allowed Brazil to only superficially integrate into globalized international production and commercial flows. The chapter concludes by providing an outlook on the policy shifts required for increasing Brazil's insertion into global value chains and boosting itself to a more prominent role in international trade.

The second chapter in this section attempts to assess if real exchange fluctuations and the demand-supply channels determined the Malaysia-China trade balances in the global crisis era, 1997–2010. The finding generally supports the complementary role of China in the Malaysia-China bilateral trading. However, despite the long-run effect of real exchange on trade balances, the Keynesian demand channel was not upheld during and after the global financial crisis—due to the contracting effect on Malaysian output. The Chinese inflation impact is also not evident following the shocks to the foreign exchanges. Meanwhile, currency devaluation for export gains is insufficient to sustain Malaysian output expansion against China. Further productivity growth in real and tradable sectors is essentially needed.

The third chapter of this section reviews and analyzes statistical data of international trade with China as well as of Chinese outbound tourism and provides an estimate of the shares Slovenia and Montenegro received. This chapter proves that China is becoming an important partner for both countries. There is a strong positive correlation between exports in China and the number of overnights of Chinese tourists both in Slovenia and Montenegro; furthermore, expenditure of Chinese tourists visiting these two countries increases every year as well.

The editor and authors of the book would like to thank InTech publishing company for the opportunity to present selected views on modern issues of international trade. This limited volume of course cannot cover all relevant questions of today's international trade. However, we believe that it will open new perspectives to interested readers.

Assoc. Prof. Anita Maček, PhD
University of Applied Sciences, FH Joanneum,
Graz, Austria

DOBA Faculty of Applied Business and Social Studies,
Maribor, Slovenia

Section 1

Selected Perspectives on International Trade

Chapter 1

Unilateral Trade Liberalization and Welfare Analysis: Iceberg Trade Costs versus Tariffs

Türkmen Göksel

Additional information is available at the end of the chapter

http://dx.doi.org/10.5772/66266

Abstract

A large body of literature in international economics has tried to explain the effect of asymmetric changes in trade barriers in welfare of the liberalizing country, however, there is no consensus on this issue. In this paper, I focus on the implications of a decline in import costs in welfare of the liberalizing country. I utilize a version of computational general equilibrium model of international trade (based on Armington assumption) where countries are potentially asymmetric in terms of labor endowment, productivity, trade barriers etc. under two different specifications of trade costs: (i) standard iceberg cost formulation and (ii) tariffs. The model numerically proves that unilateral trade liberalization is welfare improving for the liberalizing country in Armington setup with iceberg costs. However, when using tariffs, I numerically show that there exists a positive optimal tariff rate which maximizes welfare. This result indicates that a reduction in tariffs may either benefit or immiserize the liberalizing country depending on the pre-liberalization value of tariff. In the literature, a simple formula has been driven which shows the gains from trade for the case of iceberg costs. I generalize this formula in Armington setup with tariffs and highlight the importance of revenue generating tariffs.

Keywords: unilateral trade liberalization, iceberg costs, tariffs, computational general equilibrium, welfare

1. Introduction

In this paper, I focus on the implications of a decline in import costs (in terms of both iceberg costs and tariffs) in welfare[1] of the liberalizing country. There is a vast literature on the effect of asymmetric changes in trade costs in welfare of the liberalizing country; however, there is no consensus on this issue. Moreover, Eaton and Kortum (2002) [1] derive a simple formula which shows the gains from trade and this formula is generalized by Arkolakis, Costinot, and Rodriguez-Clare (2012) [2] in the case of iceberg costs. I also generalize this formula in Armington setup with tariffs and highlight the importance of revenue generating tariffs.

In Melitz [3] setup with two large but possibly asymmetric economies, unilateral trade liberalization in terms of iceberg costs is welfare improving for the liberalizing country. Similarly, in a version of the Melitz [3] model for the case of a small economy, Demidova and Rodriguez-Clare [4] also establish that welfare increases for a country that unilaterally reduces importing trade barriers in terms of iceberg costs.

These results stand in sharp contrast to two different types of models. In the first category, Felbermayr and Jung [5] show that in a two-country Melitz [3] setup, unilateral liberalization of import tariffs lowers welfare of the liberalizing country. Demidova and Rodriguez-Clare [6] also show the existence of an optimal tariff in the small economy version of the Melitz [3] model suggesting that reduction in tariffs (compared to optimal level) lowers the welfare in the liberalizing country. As mentioned in [5], the reason behind this argument is that tariffs redistribute income across countries and this generates additional leverage to the selection effect in the models with firm-level heterogeneity.

In the second category, including [7–9], trade liberalization in home country results in a welfare loss. In this category, the difference arises from the presence of an outside sector that pins down the wages. However, these setups with outside sector ignore the general equilibrium forces that are crucial for the welfare analysis. Therefore, Demidova [7], Melitz and Ottaviano [8], Ossa [9] predict immiserization for the liberalizing country due to unilateral trade liberalization. Felbermayr and Jung [5] also point out that the assumption of a linear outside sector distorts the welfare predictions of the model: In a Melitz and Ottaviano [8] setup (due to a reduction in import costs), firms in liberalizing country relocate into the relatively more protected market (outside sector) from where they serve the liberalized economy. However, in Melitz [3] (without an outside sector) setup with Pareto assumption,[2] the wage adjustment is exactly such that the relocation channel is compensated.

This paper utilizes a version of computational general equilibrium model of international trade (based on Armington assumption) where countries are possibly asymmetric in terms of labor endowment, productivity, trade costs, etc., under two different specifications: iceberg costs and tariffs. This paper aims to compute the effects of unilateral trade liberalization in welfare of the

---

[1] Given the class of models considered in this study, I use the terms welfare and real income interchangeably throughout the paper.

[2] This distributional assumption is widely used in the literature. Besides the analytical convenience of this distribution, Eaton et al. [10], among others, document that this distribution provides a reasonable approximation for the observed distribution of firm sizes.

liberalizing country in both specifications. To achieve this goal, I follow two main steps for each version. I first define and characterize the general equilibrium. In other words, I obtain a system of nonlinear equations which should be solved numerically. Second, after determining the parameters, I compute the equilibrium with numerical methods (using MATLAB). The model numerically proves that unilateral trade liberalization is welfare improving for the liberalizing country in Armington setup with iceberg costs. However, with tariffs, I numerically show that there exists a positive optimal tariff rate which maximizes welfare suggesting that a reduction in tariffs may either increase or decrease welfare of the liberalizing country depending on the pre-liberalization value of tariff.

This paper also discusses the extensions of a simple formula which is first derived by Eaton and Kortum [1] and then generalized by Arkolakis et al. [2]. These papers focus on welfare gains from trade relative to autarky in the case of iceberg costs. I generalize this formula in Armington setup with tariffs and highlight the important difference between these two formulas.

The next section presents two specifications of the model and characterizes the equilibrium for each case. Section 3 discusses the results of the numerical computations. Section 4 analytically analyzes the welfare gains from trade. Finally, Section 5 concludes.

2. Model

I utilize a version of Armington model [11–13] with two different specifications. In the first specification, I assume that trade costs are in terms of standard iceberg formulation. However, in the second case, I assume that trade costs are in terms of tariffs and tariff revenue is redistributed to the consumers in a lump-sum fashion. In both versions, there are N countries indexed by $i,j = 1,\dots,N$ where i and j denote exporters and importers, respectively. Each country has a population of measure L and I assume that all consumers are identical within countries. Armington setup is based on the assumption that each country produces a different good. Consumers in each country value not just domestically produced goods but also goods produced by foreign countries.

2.1. Model with iceberg costs

2.1.1. Demand

Country j maximizes the following constant elasticity of substitution (CES) utility function, U_j, over N goods each produced by a different country:

$$\max_{x_{ij}} U_j = \left(\sum_{i=1}^{N} \alpha_{ij}^{\frac{1}{\sigma}} x_{ij}^{\frac{\sigma-1}{\sigma}} \right)^{\frac{\sigma}{\sigma-1}} \tag{1}$$

where x_{ij} is the consumption in country j of a good produced in country i. Therefore, x_{jj} denotes the consumption of domestic good. $\alpha_{ij} > 0$ is the demand parameter that reflects the preferences of country j toward goods produced in i. The elasticity of substitution across good varieties is given by $\sigma > 1$. A higher value of σ implies goods that are more substitutable. Each consumer in country j has one unit of labor endowment which is in elastically supplied in a competitive labor market. Country j faces the following budget constraint:

$$\sum_{i=1}^{N} p_{ij}x_{ij} = w_j L_j \quad (2)$$

where p_{ij} is the price of a good produced in country i which is consumed by country j. Therefore, p_{jj} denotes the price of domestic good. w_j denotes the nominal wage in country j, and $w_j L_j$ is the total (nominal) income of country j.

The utility maximization subject to the budget constraint yields the following demand function of country j toward goods produced in i:

$$x_{ij} = \alpha_{ij}\left(\frac{p_{ij}}{P_j}\right)^{-\sigma}\frac{w_j L_j}{P_j} \quad (3)$$

where $P_j = (\sum_{i=1}^{N}\alpha_{ij}p_{ij}^{1-\sigma})^{\frac{1}{1-\sigma}}$ is the price index in country j. Note that the elasticity of substitution across good is defined as $\frac{\partial \ln\left(\frac{x_{ii}}{x_{ij}}\right)}{\partial \ln\left(\frac{p_{ii}}{p_{ij}}\right)}$. Using Eq. (3), I get the ratio of $\frac{x_{ii}}{x_{ij}}$ and by taking the logarithm of both sides, I obtain:

$$\ln\left(\frac{x_{ii}}{x_{ij}}\right) = -\sigma \ln\left(\frac{p_{ii}}{p_{ij}}\right) + (\sigma-1)\ln\left(\frac{P_i}{P_j}\right) + \ln\left(\frac{\alpha_{ii}w_i L_i}{\alpha_{ij}w_j L_j}\right) \quad (4)$$

Using Eq. (4), I simply get $\frac{\partial \ln\left(\frac{x_{ii}}{x_{ij}}\right)}{\partial \ln\left(\frac{p_{ii}}{p_{ij}}\right)} = -\sigma$. This result implies that the elasticity of substitution between good x_{ii} and x_{ij} is equal to σ.

2.1.2. Supply

Goods are produced in competitive markets. Labor is the only factor of production. In country i, there is a representative producer which has the constant returns to scale production technology: $y_{ij} = \phi_i l_{ij}$, where y_{ij} is the output produced in country i which is sold to country j, ϕ_i is the productivity level in country and l_{ij} is the labor amount used to produce good in country i in order to sell to country j. Hence, each country has potentially different productivity levels. τ_{ij} is the standard iceberg formulation of trade costs. $\tau_{ij} > 1$ implies that if one unit of good is shipped from country i to country j, only a fraction, $\frac{1}{\tau_{ij}}$, of the good arrives. There are no trade costs for domestic goods: $\tau_{ii} = 1$. Both production and trade costs are in terms of labor.

The profit maximization of a representative producer in country i when selling to country j is given by:

$$\max_{x_{ij}} p_{ij} x_{ij} - \frac{w_i x_{ij} \tau_{ij}}{\phi_i} \tag{5}$$

The profit maximization in competitive markets yields the following price rule:

$$p_{ij} = \frac{w_i \tau_{ij}}{\phi_i} \tag{6}$$

2.1.3. *Equilibrium conditions*

In order to fully characterize the equilibrium, one needs two more conditions. I first consider the labor market clearing condition. This condition implies that labor supply has to be equal to the total labor demand in country *i*. Hence, labor market clearing condition for country *i* can be written as:

$$L_i = \sum_{j=1}^{N} \frac{x_{ij} \tau_{ij}}{\phi_i} \tag{7}$$

Second equilibrium condition is the balanced trade condition. This condition implies that the value of total imports has to be equal to the value of total exports of country *i*. Balanced trade condition for country *i* can be written as:

$$\sum_{j=1(i\neq j)}^{N} p_{ij} x_{ij} = \sum_{j=1(i\neq j)}^{N} p_{ji} x_{ji} \tag{8}$$

2.1.4. *Characterization of equilibrium*

The equilibrium is characterized by N^2 demand equations, N labor market clearing conditions and $\frac{N^2-N}{2}$ balanced trade equations. Hence, in total, one needs $\frac{3N^2+N}{2}$ equations to characterize the equilibrium. In particular, for a two-country model $(N = 2)$, the seven equilibrium equations are given by:

$$x_{11} = \alpha_{11} \left(\frac{p_{11}}{P_1}\right)^{-\sigma} \frac{w_1 L_1}{P_1} \tag{9}$$

$$x_{12} = \alpha_{12} \left(\frac{p_{12}}{P_2}\right)^{-\sigma} \frac{w_2 L_2}{P_2} \tag{10}$$

$$x_{22} = \alpha_{22} \left(\frac{p_{22}}{P_2}\right)^{-\sigma} \frac{w_2 L_2}{P_2} \tag{11}$$

$$x_{21} = \alpha_{21} \left(\frac{p_{21}}{P_1}\right)^{-\sigma} \frac{w_1 L_1}{P_1} \tag{12}$$

$$L_1 = \frac{x_{11} \tau_{11}}{\phi_1} + \frac{x_{12} \tau_{12}}{\phi_1} \tag{13}$$

$$L_2 = \frac{x_{21}\tau_{21}}{\phi_2} + \frac{x_{22}\tau_{22}}{\phi_2} \tag{14}$$

$$p_{21}x_{21} = p_{12}x_{12} \tag{15}$$

However, the given system has twelve unknown variables: eight prices ($p_{11}, p_{12}, p_{21}, p_{22}, w_1, w_2, P_1, P_2$) and four consumption quantities ($x_{11}, x_{12}, x_{21}, x_{22}$), but only seven equations. By using the definition of price index $P_j = (\sum_{i=1}^{N} \alpha_{ij} p_{ij}^{1-\sigma})^{\frac{1}{1-\sigma}}$, the solution of profit maximization problem $p_{ij} = \frac{w_i \tau_{ij}}{\phi_i}$ and normalizing one of the prices, (p_{22}), to one, the equilibrium is characterized by a system of seven unknowns and seven equations:

$$x_{11} = \alpha_{11} p_{11}^{-\sigma} \frac{w_1 L_1}{\alpha_{11} p_{11}^{1-\sigma} + \alpha_{21} \tau_{21}^{1-\sigma}} \tag{16}$$

$$x_{12} = \alpha_{12} (p_{11}\tau_{12})^{-\sigma} \frac{w_2 L_2}{\alpha_{22} + \alpha_{12} (p_{11}\tau_{12})^{1-\sigma}} \tag{17}$$

$$x_{22} = \alpha_{22} \frac{w_2 L_2}{\alpha_{22} + \alpha_{12} (p_{11}\tau_{12})^{1-\sigma}} \tag{18}$$

$$x_{21} = \alpha_{21} \tau_{21}^{-\sigma} \frac{w_1 L_1}{\alpha_{11} p_{11}^{1-\sigma} + \alpha_{21} \tau_{21}^{1-\sigma}} \tag{19}$$

$$L_1 = \frac{x_{11}}{\phi_1} + \frac{x_{12}\tau_{12}}{\phi_1} \tag{20}$$

$$L_2 = \frac{x_{21}\tau_{21}}{\phi_2} + \frac{x_{22}}{\phi_2} \tag{21}$$

$$\tau_{21} x_{21} = p_{11} \tau_{12} x_{12} \tag{22}$$

Given the value of parameters and price normalization, one has to solve for three prices (p_{11}, w_1, w_2) and four consumption quantities ($x_{11}, x_{12}, x_{21}, x_{22}$). I use MATLAB in order to solve this nonlinear equation system.

2.2. Model with tariffs

2.2.1. Demand

Now, I assume that trade barriers are in terms of tariffs rather than iceberg trade costs. In this setup, tariff revenue from imports is redistributed to the consumers in a lump-sum fashion. The only change in country *j*'s utility maximization problem is the budget constraint:

$$\sum_{i=1}^{N} p_{ij} x_{ij} = w_j L_j + T_j \tag{23}$$

where T_j represents the tariff revenue of country *j*.

The utility maximization subject to this new budget constraint yields the following demand equation:

$$x_{ij} = \alpha_{ij}\left(\frac{p_{ij}}{P_j}\right)^{-\sigma}\frac{w_jL_j + T_j}{P_j} \tag{24}$$

where $P_j = (\sum_{i=1}^{N}\alpha_{ij}p_{ij}^{1-\sigma})^{\frac{1}{1-\sigma}}$ is the price index in country *j*.

2.2.2. Supply

The only change in firm's problem is that τ_{ij} is treated as tariffs rather than iceberg costs. Tariffs are rebated lump sum to the consumers. The solution for profit maximization of a representative producer in country *i* when selling to country *j* in competitive markets is unchanged:

$$p_{ij} = \frac{w_i\tau_{ij}}{\phi_i} \tag{25}$$

2.2.3. Equilibrium conditions

In order to fully characterize the equilibrium, one needs three conditions: labor market clearing condition, the balanced trade condition and the tariff revenue that has to be fully redistributed to the consumers.

Labor market clearing implies that labor supply in country has to be equal to the total labor demand in country *i*:

$$L_i = \sum_{j=1}^{N}\frac{x_{ij}}{\phi_i} \tag{26}$$

Note that in contrast to the iceberg formulation, there are no additional production and employment for tariffs. Second equilibrium condition is the balanced trade condition. This condition implies that the value of total imports has to be equal to the value of total exports of country *i*. Balanced trade condition for country *i* can be written as

$$\sum_{j=1(i\neq j)}^{N}\frac{p_{ij}x_{ij}}{\tau_{ij}} = \sum_{j=1(i\neq j)}^{N}\frac{p_{ji}x_{ji}}{\tau_{ji}} \tag{27}$$

where dividing by τ_{ij} takes care of $p_{ij}x_{ij}$ being defined as inclusive of tariffs. Note that $p_{ij}x_{ij}$ is the value of imports of country *j* from *i* inclusive of tariffs. However, $\frac{p_{ij}x_{ij}}{\tau_{ij}}$ is the value of imports exclusive of tariffs.

Finally, tariff revenue in country *j* is given by:

$$T_j = p_{ij}x_{ij}(\tau_{ij}-1) \tag{28}$$

2.2.4. Characterization of equilibrium

Consider a two-country ($N = 2$) case. Normalizing one of the prices, p_{22}, to one, the equilibrium is characterized by a system of nine unknowns and nine equations:

$$x_{11} = \alpha_{11} p_{11}^{-\sigma} \frac{w_1 L_1 + T_1}{\alpha_{11} p_{11}^{1-\sigma} + \alpha_{21} \tau_{21}^{1-\sigma}} \tag{29}$$

$$x_{12} = \alpha_{12} (p_{11} \tau_{12})^{-\sigma} \frac{w_2 L_2 + T_2}{\alpha_{22} + \alpha_{12} (p_{11} \tau_{12})^{1-\sigma}} \tag{30}$$

$$x_{22} = \alpha_{22} \frac{w_2 L_2 + T_2}{\alpha_{22} + \alpha_{12} (p_{11} \tau_{12})^{1-\sigma}} \tag{31}$$

$$x_{21} = \alpha_{21} \tau_{21}^{-\sigma} \frac{w_1 L_1 + T_1}{\alpha_{11} p_{11}^{1-\sigma} + \alpha_{21} \tau_{21}^{1-\sigma}} \tag{32}$$

$$L_1 = \frac{x_{11}}{\phi_1} + \frac{x_{12}}{\phi_1} \tag{33}$$

$$L_2 = \frac{x_{21}}{\phi_2} + \frac{x_{22}}{\phi_2} \tag{34}$$

$$p_{22} x_{21} = p_{11} x_{12} \tag{35}$$

$$T_1 = p_{22} x_{21} (\tau_{21} - 1) \tag{36}$$

$$T_2 = p_{11} x_{12} (\tau_{12} - 1) \tag{37}$$

Given the value of parameters and price normalization, one has to solve for three prices (p_{11}, w_1, w_2), four consumption quantities ($x_{11}, x_{12}, x_{21}, x_{22}$) and tariff revenue for both countries, T_1 and T_2.

3. Numerical exercises: unilateral trade liberalization

3.1. Iceberg costs

Consider two symmetric countries: home (country 1) and foreign (country 2). Main goal of this section is to compute the effects of unilateral trade liberalization (at home) in welfare. In a benchmark model, I assume that $\tau_{12} = \tau_{21} = 1.2$. In the counterfactual analysis, I set import barriers in terms of iceberg costs for home country (τ_{21}) to 1 keeping τ_{12} unchanged. **Table 1** presents the parameter values which are used in numerical computations.

For the trade elasticity, I follow Anderson and Van Wincoop [14]. Anderson and Van Wincoop [14] suggest that the value for trade elasticity (ε) lies in the range of $[-10, -5]$ after a

http://dx.doi.org/10.5772/66266

comprehensive review of the existing literature. In our Armington setup, trade elasticity, ε, is equal to one minus elasticity of substitution across goods, $1-\sigma$.[3] In the numeric computations, I choose a value of 8 for σ in order to match $\varepsilon = -7$.

	Benchmark model	Counterfactual analysis
L_1	1	1
L_2	1	1
ϕ_1	1	1
ϕ_2	1	1
σ	8	8
α_{11}	0.6	0.6
α_{12}	0.4	0.4
α_{21}	0.4	0.4
α_{22}	0.6	0.6
τ_{11}	1	1
τ_{12}	1.2	1.2
τ_{21}	1.2	1
τ_{22}	1	1

Table 1. Parameter values.

Table 2 presents the computation results of both exercises: benchmark model and counterfactual analysis.

Computation results in **Table 2** imply that unilateral reduction in iceberg costs in country 1 increases the welfare in country 1. The mechanism is as follows: A decrease in import trade barriers in country 1 reduces the price of the imported good in country 1 which yields an increase in imports from country 2. To restore trade balance nominal wages in country should fall and this causes a decline in the price of domestic goods. The reduction in both prices (domestic and import) yields a reduction in aggregate price index in country 1 as well. The decrease in price index dominates the decrease in nominal wages and therefore, real income (welfare) in country 1 is increasing. Moreover, the unilateral reduction in iceberg costs in country 1 causes an increase in real income of country 2. However, the increase in country 2 is smaller than the increase in country 1.

Figure 1 depicts the welfare changes associated with unilateral trade liberalization (in terms of iceberg costs) in country 1 keeping $\tau_{12} = 1.2$ unchanged.

In **Figure 1**, I conclude that trade liberalization (in the case of iceberg costs) monotonically increases the welfare of the liberalizing country.

[3]This result is proven in Section 4.

	Benchmark model (I)	Counterfactual analysis (II)	(II)/(I)
p_{11}	1	0.9202	0.9202
p_{12}	1.2	1.1043	0.9202
p_{21}	1.2	1	0.8333
p_{22}	1	1	1
w_1	1	0.9202	0.9202
w_2	1	1	1
P_1	1.0498	0.9461	0.9012
P_2	1.0498	1.0324	0.9834
Welfare_1	0.9526	0.9726	1.0210
Welfare_2	0.9526	0.9686	1.0167
Exports/GDP_1	15.69%	27.14%	1.7297
Imports/GDP_1	15.69%	27.14%	1.7297
Exports/GDP_2	15.69%	24.98%	1.5920
Imports/GDP_2	15.69%	24.98%	1.5920

Table 2. Computation results.

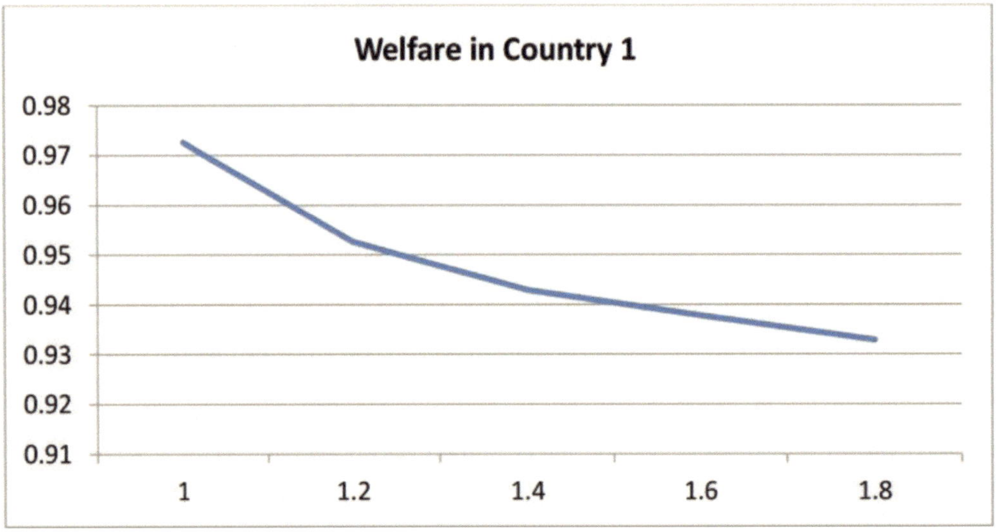

Figure 1. Welfare changes associated with unilateral trade liberalization (in terms of iceberg costs) in country 1.

3.2. Tariffs

Using the same parameters in **Table 1** for the benchmark and counterfactual analyses, **Table 3** presents the computation results of both exercises in the case of tariffs. Exports and imports values are presented in both ways (inclusive and exclusive in tariffs).

http://dx.doi.org/10.5772/66266

	Benchmark model (I)	Counterfactual analysis (II)	(II)/(I)
p_{11}	1	0.9092	0.9092
p_{12}	1.2	1.0910	0.9091
p_{21}	1.2	1	0.8333
p_{22}	1	1	1
w_1	1	0.9092	0.9092
w_2	1	1	1
P_1	1.0498	0.9377	0.8932
P_2	1.0498	1.0292	0.9803
Welfare_1	0.9781	0.9696	0.9913
Welfare_2	0.9781	1.0167	1.0394
Exports/GDP_1	13.07%	25.51%	1.9517
Imports/GDP_1	13.07%	25.51%	1.9517
Exports/GDP_2	13.07%	22.16%	1.6954
Imports/GDP_2	13.07%	22.16%	1.6954
Exports/GDP_1*	15.68%	25.51%	1.6269
Imports/GDP_1*	15.68%	25.51%	1.6269
Exports/GDP_2*	15.68%	22.16%	1.4132
Imports/GDP_2*	15.68%	22.16%	1.4132
Tariff revenue_1	0.0268	0	0
Tariff revenue_2	0.0268	0.0464	1.7313
Tariff $\text{revenue}_1/\text{GDP}_1$	2.61%	0%	0
Tariff $\text{revenue}_2/\text{GDP}_2$	2.61%	4.43%	1.6973
Tariff multiplier_1	1.0268	1	0.9738
Tariff multiplier_2	1.0268	1.0464	1.0190

* Inclusive of tariffs.

Table 3. Computation results.

In contrast to the iceberg cost formulation, unilateral trade liberalization causes a welfare loss in the liberalizing country 1. However, this result depends on pre-liberalization value of tariffs. **Figure 2** shows the welfare changes associated with unilateral trade liberalization in country 1 (in terms of tariffs) keeping $\tau_{12} = 1.2$ unchanged.

Figure 2 also implies that there exists an optimal positive tariff rate (which maximizes welfare) which is around 20% in our case.

3.3. Discussion: iceberg costs versus tariffs

Numerical solutions suggest that in Armington setup, iceberg cost and tariff formulations give the different welfare implications. Therefore, the type of trade barrier plays a crucial role in computing the welfare gains due to trade liberalization. This result can be generalized (see [1, 3, 15, 16] for details).

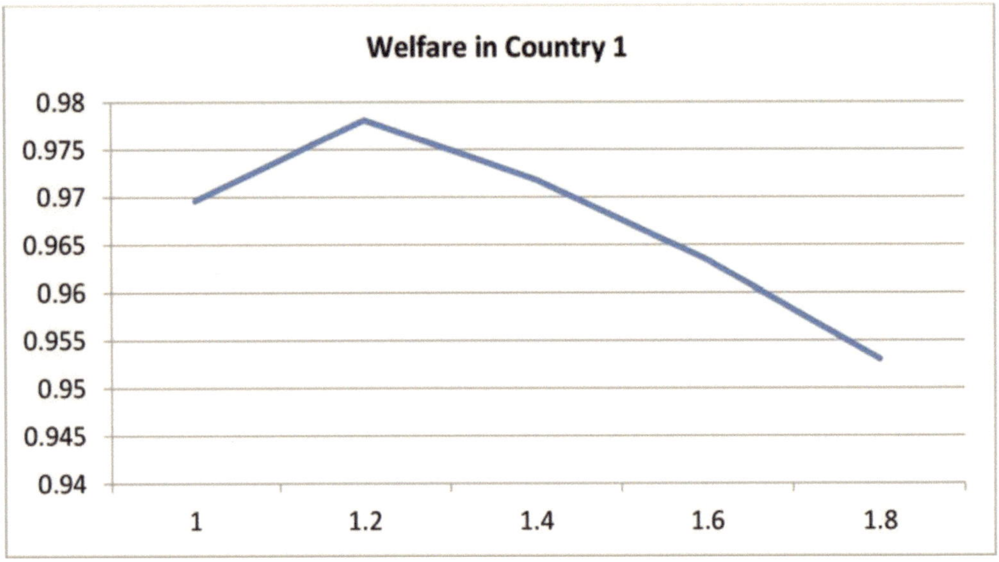

Figure 2. Welfare changes associated with unilateral trade liberalization (in terms of tariffs) in country 1.

Similar to my findings, Felbermayr and Jung [5] show that in a two-country Melitz [3] setup, unilateral liberalization of import tariffs lowers welfare of the liberalizing country. Demidova and Rodriguez-Clare [6] also show the existence of an optimal tariff in the small economy version of the Melitz [3] model, suggesting that reduction in tariffs (compared to optimal level) lowers the welfare in liberalizing country.

4. Gains from trade: welfare analysis

Eaton and Kortum [1] show that welfare gains from trade are function of only two elements in the case of iceberg costs: (i) the share of expenditure on domestic goods, which is equal to one minus the import penetration ratio and (ii) trade elasticity (an elasticity of imports with respect to variable iceberg trade costs). This result is generalized by Arkolakis et al. [2] for a large class of trade models, including the one used in this paper (version of Armington model), Eaton and Kortum [1], Krugman [15] and Melitzs [3] models in the case of iceberg costs.[4] This generalized result implies that although recent quantitative trade models can explain a wider set of micro-

[4]The Frechet and the Parteo distributions are considered for productivities in Eaton and Kortum [1] and Melitz [3] frameworks, respectively.

level facts, all type of models mentioned above calculate the exact same amount of gains from trade in the case of iceberg costs. In summary, welfare gains from trade liberalization do not depend on the different models microstructure.[5]

However, this paper argues that the result generalized by Arkolakis et al. [2] is only true in the case of iceberg costs, but not in the tariff formulation, since the formula generalized by Arkolakis et al. [2] ignores the tariff redistribution.

Section 4.1 derives the simple formula which is generalized by Arkolakis et al. [2] in the case of iceberg costs. Section 4.2 extends the simple formula in the case of tariffs and highlights the important difference between two formulas.

4.1. Simple formula for the gains from trade: iceberg cost formulation

Arkolakis et al. [2] generalized a simple formula for the gains from trade for a large set of trade models including Armington [11], Krugman [15], Eaton and Kortum [1] and Melitz [3] models in the case of iceberg costs. In order to compute the gains from trade by this simple formula, one only needs two elements: (i) the share of expenditure on domestic goods (λ_{jj}) and (ii) elasticity of imports with respect to iceberg costs, ($1-\sigma$).

Using our model in Section 3, let's first show that trade elasticity (elasticity of imports with respect to iceberg costs) which is defined as $\frac{\partial \ln(X_{ij}/X_{jj})}{\partial ln\tau_{ij}}$ is equal to ($1-\sigma$). Second, one can write the share of expenditure on domestic goods, λ_{jj}, just in terms of prices. Finally, one can relate these two elements with welfare (real income) definition $W_j = \frac{w_j}{P_j}$ in country j.

For the first step, let's write the equation for imports of country j from country i:

$$x_{ij} = \alpha_{ij}\left(\frac{p_{ij}}{P_j}\right)^{-\sigma}\frac{w_jL_j}{P_j} \tag{38}$$

Let's multiply both sides by p_{ij} in order to get the value of imports (rather than quantities) of country j from country i which is denoted by X_{ij}:

$$X_{ij} = \alpha_{ij}\left(\frac{p_{ij}}{P_j}\right)^{1-\sigma} w_jL_j \tag{39}$$

Let's derive X_{ij}/X_{jj} by using the equality of $p_{ij} = \frac{w_i\tau_{ij}}{\phi_i}$ (recall that $\tau_{jj} = 1$):

[5]Arkolakis et al. [2] discuss some extensions of their result. Adding multiple sectors, tradable intermediate goods or multiple factors of production into the model can change the validity of their result. In particular, Balistreri et al. [17] add a second non-tradable sector and they show that models with perfect and monopolistic competition no longer have the same welfare implications.

$$\frac{X_{ij}}{X_{jj}} = \frac{\alpha_{ij}}{\alpha_{jj}} \left(\frac{w_i}{w_j} \frac{\phi_j}{\phi_i} \tau_{ij} \right)^{1-\sigma} \tag{40}$$

Taking the natural logarithm of both sides of Eq. (40), I obtain:

$$ln\left(\frac{X_{ij}}{X_{jj}}\right) = ln\left(\frac{\alpha_{ij}}{\alpha_{jj}}\right) + (1-\sigma)ln\left(\frac{w_i}{w_j} \frac{\phi_j}{\phi_i}\right) + (1-\sigma)ln(\tau_{ij}) \tag{41}$$

By using Eq. (41), after the simple math, I get:

$$\frac{\partial \ln\left(\frac{X_{ij}}{X_{jj}}\right)}{\partial ln\tau_{ij}} = (1-\sigma) \tag{42}$$

Hence, the trade elasticity (elasticity of imports with respect to iceberg costs) is equal to one minus elasticity of substitution across good varieties.

For the second step, I use the definition $\lambda_{jj} \equiv \frac{X_{jj}}{\sum_{i=1}^{N} X_{ij}}$. Using Eq. (39) and $\sum_{i=1}^{N} X_{ij} = w_j L_j$ equality, I can rewrite this equation as follows:

$$\lambda_{jj} = \frac{\alpha_{jj} \left(\frac{p_{jj}}{P_j}\right)^{1-\sigma} w_j L_j}{w_j L_j} = \alpha_{jj} \left(\frac{p_{jj}}{P_j}\right)^{1-\sigma} \tag{43}$$

After solving for $\frac{p_{jj}}{P_j}$, I obtain:

$$\frac{p_{jj}}{P_j} = \left(\frac{\lambda_{jj}}{\alpha_{jj}}\right)^{\frac{1}{1-\sigma}} \tag{44}$$

For the final step, let's define welfare in country j, W_j, which is measured by the real income $\frac{w_j}{P_j}$. Using the $p_{jj} = \frac{w_j}{\phi_j}$ result (recall that $\tau_{jj} = 1$), I can rewrite the real income as:

$$\frac{w_j}{P_j} = \frac{p_{jj} \phi_j}{P_j} \tag{45}$$

Finally, by substituting $\frac{p_{jj}}{P_j} = \left(\frac{\lambda_{jj}}{\alpha_{jj}}\right)^{\frac{1}{1-\sigma}}$ into the Eq. (45), I get W_j as follows:

$$W_j = \frac{w_j}{P_j} = \lambda_{jj}^{\frac{1}{1-\sigma}} \alpha_{jj}^{\frac{1}{\sigma-1}} \phi_j \tag{46}$$

Welfare gains from trade can be shown as the change in welfare before and after trade:

http://dx.doi.org/10.5772/66266

$$\frac{\hat{W}_j}{W_j} = \frac{\hat{\lambda}_{jj}^{\frac{1}{1-\sigma}} \alpha_{jj}^{\frac{1}{\sigma-1}} \phi_j}{\lambda_{jj}^{\frac{1}{1-\sigma}} \alpha_{jj}^{\frac{1}{\sigma-1}} \phi_j} = \left(\frac{\hat{\lambda}_{jj}}{\lambda_{jj}}\right)^{\frac{1}{1-\sigma}} \tag{47}$$

where $\hat{W}_j$ and W_j denote welfare after and before trade, respectively. Since I focus on trade liberalization, I assume that there is no change in other parameters such as α_{jj} and ϕ_j. I conclude that to compute the change in welfare due to trade liberalization, one only needs to know the change in share of expenditure on domestic goods and trade elasticity, $\varepsilon = 1\text{–}\sigma$.

Let's apply our formula to the numerical exercise in Section 3.1 for country 1. 0.1569 and 0.2714 are the share of imports to GDP before and after unilateral trade liberalization (reduction in τ_{21} from 1.2 to 1), respectively. Hence, I get 1 – 0.1569 = 0.8431 before trade liberalization and 1 – 0.2714 = 0.7286 after trade liberalization as the share of expenditures on domestic goods. In Section 3, I assume that the elasticity of substitution across good is eight suggesting a value of –7 ($\varepsilon = 1\text{–}8 = \text{–}7$) for the trade elasticity. Now, let's substitute these values into our simple formula:

$$\frac{\hat{W}_j}{W_j} = \left(\frac{\hat{\lambda}_{jj}}{\lambda_{jj}}\right)^{\frac{1}{1-\sigma}} = \left(\frac{0.7286}{0.8431}\right)^{\frac{1}{1-8}} = 1.0210 \tag{48}$$

National income in country 1 increased by 2.1% due to unilateral trade liberalization which is the same result I obtain in **Table 2**.

4.2. Simple formula for the gains from trade: tariff formulation

This section extends the simple formula derived by Arkolakis et al. [2]. In this section, I assume that trade barriers are in the form of tariffs rather than iceberg costs. In order to compute the gains from trade by the extended formula, one needs three elements rather than two: (i) the share of expenditure on domestic goods (λ_{jj}), (ii) elasticity of imports with respect to tariffs (1–σ) and (iii) a tariff multiplier (β_j).

Applying the similar steps with the previous section (the case of iceberg costs), I obtain the same equation for $\frac{p_{jj}}{P_j}$ in the case of tariffs:

$$\frac{p_{jj}}{P_j} = \left(\frac{\lambda_{jj}}{\alpha_{jj}}\right)^{\frac{1}{1-\sigma}} \tag{49}$$

However, in the case of tariff, total income in country j is $X_j = w_j L_j + T_j$ rather than just $w_j L_j$. Now, let's drive the tariff multiplier, β_j, for country j. By definition, I have:

$$X_j \equiv X_j \tag{50}$$

Multiplying RHS by $\frac{w_j L_j}{w_j L_j}$, I obtain:

$$X_j \equiv X_j \frac{w_j L_j}{w_j L_j} \tag{51}$$

Since I know that $w_j L_j = X_j - T_j$

$$X_j \equiv X_j \frac{w_j L_j}{X_j - T_j} \tag{52}$$

Hence, I have:

$$X_j = \beta_j w_j L_j \tag{53}$$

where $\beta_j = \frac{X_j}{X_j - T_j}$ is the tariff multiplier. Since $X_j - T_j < X_j$ with positive tariff revenues, multiplier β_j takes values >1. I can rewrite β_j as $\left(1 - \frac{T_j}{X_j}\right)^{-1}$ which is the inverse of one minus the share of tariffs in total income. Hence, it is enough to know the share of tariffs in total income in order to compute the tariff multiplier. Given the tariff multiplier, the real income is equal to $\beta_j \frac{w_j}{P_j}$. Using the $p_{jj} = \frac{w_j}{\phi_j}$ result (recall that $\tau_{jj} = 1$), one can rewrite the real wage as:

$$\beta_j \frac{w_j}{P_j} = \beta_j \frac{p_{jj} \phi_j}{P_j} \tag{54}$$

Finally, by substituting $\frac{p_{jj}}{P_j} = \left(\frac{\lambda_{jj}}{\alpha_{jj}}\right)^{\frac{1}{1-\sigma}}$ into Eq. (54), I get W_j as follows:

$$W_j = \beta_j \frac{w_j}{P_j} = \beta_j \lambda_{jj}^{\frac{1}{1-\sigma}} \alpha_{jj}^{\frac{1}{\sigma-1}} \phi_j \tag{55}$$

Welfare gains from trade can be shown as the change in welfare before and after trade:

$$\frac{\hat{W}_j}{W_j} = \frac{\hat{\beta}_j \hat{\lambda}_{jj}^{\frac{1}{1-\sigma}} \alpha_{jj}^{\frac{1}{\sigma-1}} \phi_j}{\beta_j \lambda_{jj}^{\frac{1}{1-\sigma}} \alpha_{jj}^{\frac{1}{\sigma-1}} \phi_j} = \frac{\hat{\beta}_j}{\beta_j} \left(\frac{\hat{\lambda}_{jj}}{\lambda_{jj}}\right)^{\frac{1}{1-\sigma}} \tag{56}$$

where $\hat{W}_j$ and W_j denote welfare after and before trade, respectively. Since I focus on trade liberalization, I assume that there is no change in other parameters such as α_{jj} and ϕ_j. I conclude that to compute the change in welfare due to trade liberalization, one only needs to know changes in share of expenditure on domestic goods, trade elasticity and the tariff multiplier.

Let's apply our formula to the numerical exercise in Section 3.2 for country 1. 0.1568 and 0.2551 are the share of imports to GDP (inclusive of tariffs) before and after unilateral trade liberalization (reduction in τ_{21} from 1.2 to 1), respectively, in the case of tariffs. Hence, I get 1 – 0.1568 = 0.8432 before trade liberalization and 1 – 0.2551 = 0.7449 after trade liberalization as the share of expenditures on domestic goods. In Section 3, I assume that the elasticity of substitution across good is 8 suggesting a value of −7 for the trade elasticity. Now, let's substitute these values into our simple formula and I obtain:

$$\frac{\hat{W}_j}{W_j} = \left(\frac{\hat{\lambda}_{jj}}{\lambda_{jj}}\right)^{\frac{1}{1-\sigma}} \frac{\hat{\beta}_j}{\beta_j} = \left(\frac{0.7449}{0.8432}\right)^{\frac{1}{1-8}} \frac{1}{1.0268} = 0.9913 \tag{57}$$

National income in country 1 decreased due to unilateral trade liberalization which is the same result I obtain in **Table 3**.

5. Conclusion

Although there is a fairly sizable literature in international trade, there is no general agreement on the implications of unilateral trade liberalization in welfare of the liberalizing country. This paper studies the effects of a decline in import costs (in terms of both iceberg cost and tariffs) in welfare of the liberalizing country. Based on Armington model, I numerically show that unilateral trade liberalization is welfare improving for the liberalizing country in the case of iceberg costs. However, in the tariff case, I numerically show that there exists a positive optimal tariff rate which maximizes welfare, suggesting that a reduction in tariffs may either increases or decreases welfare of liberalizing country depending on the pre-liberalization value of tariff.

Moreover, this paper also discusses the welfare gains from trade with a simple equation which is derived by Eaton and Kortum [1] and generalized by Arkolakis et al. [2] in the case of iceberg costs. I generalize this formula in Armington setup with tariffs and highlight the importance of revenue-generating tariffs.

Author details

Türkmen Göksel

Address all correspondence to: tgoksel@ankara.edu.tr

Department of Economics, Ankara University, Turkey

References

[1] Eaton J, Kortum S. Technology, geography and trade. Econometrica. 2002;70(5):1741–1779.

[2] Arkolakis C, Costinot A, Rodriguez-Clare A. New trade models, same old gains? American Economic Review. 2012;102(1):94–130.

[3] Melitz MJ. The impact of trade on intra-industry reallocations and aggregate industry productivity. Econometrica. 2003;71:1695–1725.

[4] Demidova S, Rodriguez-Clare A. The simple analytics of the Melitz model in a small open economy. Journal of International Economics. 2013;90:266–272.

[5] Felbermayr G, Jung B. Unilateral trade liberalization in the Melitz model: a note. Economics Bulletin. 2012;32(2):1724–1730.

[6] Demidova S, Rodriguez-Clare A. Trade policy under firm-level heterogeneity in a small open economy. Journal of International Economics. 2009;78(1):100–112.

[7] Demidova S. Productivity improvements and falling trade costs: boon or bane. International Economic Review. 2008;49(4):1437–1462.

[8] Melitz MJ, Ottaviano GIP. Market size, trade and productivity. Review of Economic Studies. 2008;75(1):295–316.

[9] Ossa R. A new trade theory of GATT/WTO Negotiations. Journal of Political Economy. 2011;119(1):12–152.

[10] Eaton J, Kortum S, Kramarz F. An anatomy of international trade: evidence from French firms. Econometrica. 2011;79(5):1453–1498.

[11] Armington PS. A theory of demand for products distinguished by place of production. International Monetary Fund Staff Papers. 1969;16(1):170–201.

[12] Anderson JE. A theoretical foundation for the gravity equation. The American Review. 1979;69(1):106–116.

[13] Anderson JE, Van Wincoop E. Gravity with gravitas: a solution to the border puzzle. The American Economic Review. 2003;93(1):170–192.

[14] Anderson JE, Van Wincoop E. Trade costs. Journal of Economic Literature. 2004;42 (3):691–751.

[15] Krugman P. Scale economies, product differentiation and the pattern of trade. The American Economic Review. 1980;70(5):950–959.

[16] Felbermayr G, Jung B, Larch M. Optimal tariffs, retaliation and the welfare loss from tariff wars in the Melitz model. Journal of International Economics. 2013;89(1):13–25.

[17] Balistreri EJ, Hillberry RH, Rutherford TH. Trade and welfare: Does industrial organization matter? Economics Letter. 2010;109(2):85–87.

Chapter 2

Globalization, Governance, Democratization and Fair Trade

Rasto Ovin and Pedja Ašanin Gole

Additional information is available at the end of the chapter

http://dx.doi.org/10.5772/66370

Abstract

The chapter presents the discussion on fair trade initiatives and their possible role in achieving more equilibrated trade relations inside globalization and governance. The authors want to challenge the overrated goodwill of peoples' initiative mostly positioning itself as a counterpart of existing trade policy developments. Fair trade is scanned through principles of economics, which enable a conclusion that the present concept is too narrow to produce enough inside energy for its establishment in real policy of developed economies. Special attention the authors are paying to governance as a field that may profoundly explain the gaps subject to action in the fair trade initiatives. Due to the global meaning of the principle for sustainable global trade and security, it must continuously be more and more incorporated in the mainstream politics of world leading economies.

Keywords: trade policy, fair trade, NGOs, economics of trade, economic policy, governance, globalization

1. Introduction

Although being an element of sustainable economics—related to regional policy—fair trade has been discussed and explained primarily from the position of civilization development goals and is subject to mainly soft approach of governance. It is, of course, the role of progressive individuals and NGOs to point to the areas, which should enter mainstream government policies' perspectives. On the other hand, however, the ability to act for the solution of the problem is not on the side of such pluralist approach. These are governments of leading economies, who should adopt principles of fair trade, as they are in the line of the contemporary level of civilization as well as a must for creation of sustainable global trade environment.

Unlike partial knowledge and perspective of individual fair trade promoters, the governments dispose of overbroad and direct access to information, resources and tools to act in support of fair trade.

With the help of comparative approach in this chapter, we are pointing to the fact that fair trade is a necessary route to make international trade sustainable, and we are trying to explain why it will remain the competence and responsibility of governments in industrial economies. The main argument of this chapter is that present fair trade initiatives lack fundaments of economics as well as of the theory of economic policy. While the first one requires much broader definition and impact of the fair trade, the second poses inevitable requirements for the level that can make this concept work.

2. Economics of fair trade

The basic principle of regional policy is that underdeveloped regions will get the opportunity to catch up with the developed regions when (if) there will be trade among them. Deepening of trade relations will help to engage underdeveloped regions in economic areas together with industrial economies. Including this principle means to automatically exclude the trade based on exploration of undeveloped regions' resources and to include the sustainability principle. The sustainability risk of such 'unfair trade' for developed economies appears in three forms. The first one is that oppression of trade partners and prices of exporters to industrial economies leads to cost and price competition that at the end cannot be sustained by developed economies themselves. The second one refers to the need of transfer campaigns to help underdeveloped regions (states). They usually serve only for the pacification of certain states or groups that threaten to bring destruction to established trade and security context. The third form has been demonstrated with recent immigration developments in the EU. According to European Commission Vice President Frans Timmermans [1], it is assessed that 60% of immigrants are moving for economic reasons—thus it is not difficult to recognize the pattern, which may prevail if the population's perspective in low-income countries will not develop.

It has not been proved anything else that humans react to economic stimulations in a pattern that partially resembles laws of physics. Here it is enough to mention the laws on prices and quantities of supply and demand. It is, however, a requirement of civilization stance and sustainability as discussed above to promote institutional arrangements for assuring opportunities for states and groups, who were deprived of their political and economic development.

3. Fair trade terminology and present developments

The term 'fair trade' is a generic concept. The World Fair Trade Organization as a global network of fair trade organizations defines fair trade as 'a trading partnership, based on dialogue, transparency and respect, which seeks greater equity in international trade. It contributes to sustainable development by offering better trading conditions to, and securing the rights of, marginalised producers and workers, especially in the South. Fair Trade Organizations (backed by consumers) are engaged actively in supporting producers, awareness raising and in campaigning for changes in the rules and practice of conventional international trade' [2, 3].

Fair trade is also an international movement to socially regulate global markets (particularly in the food sector) who seeks to empower producers in the global South (through the provision of better prices, stable market links and development resources) and to promote responsible consumption and provide shoppers with socially and environmentally friendly products in the global North. This movement is therefore a favour of social and environmental justice and develops alternative economic spaces of production, trade, retailing and consumption. According to Encyclopedia of Political Theory [4], 'the goals of the fair trade movement include improving the livelihoods and well-being of small producers; promoting development opportunities for disadvantaged groups of producers, in particular women and indigenous people; raising awareness among consumers of the negative effects of patterns of international trade on producers in the Global South; campaigning for changes in the regulatory regimes governing international trade; and the protection and promotion of human rights. The international fair trade movement consists of certification agencies, producer organizations and cooperatives, trading networks, and retailers'.

The explanation of the term 'fair trade' by the Fairtrade Foundation reads: 'With fair trade you have the power to change the world every day. With simple shopping choices, you can get farmers a better deal. And that means they can make their own decisions, control their futures and lead the dignified life everyone deserves' [5]. Such explanation is not only normative but is also vague and is subject to historical anthropomorphism to such extent that it cannot be used for economic analysis.

Somewhat clearer is the description of fair trade as 'organized social movement and market—based approach that aims to help producers in developing countries to make better trading conditions and promote sustainability. The movement advocates the payment of higher prices to exporters as well as higher social and environmental standards. It focuses in particular on exports from developing countries to develop countries, most notably handicrafts, coffee, cocoa, sugar, tea, bananas, honey, cotton, wine, fresh fruit, chocolate, flowers and gold' [6, 7]. Basing on the role of trade in reducing regional differences, we believe that the established concept of fair trade as presented above is simple to narrow. If we recognize the ricochet effects of unfair trade for developed economies, we simply should understand fair trade as an element of sustainable trade and of economics in a broader sense.

Therefore, we are underlining our disagreement with the interpretation that the fair trade concept refers only to developing economies and regions. It is a minimum requirement to see a broad picture, where disequilibria in global trade are taking us in the era of almost unlimited mobility of information and resources. Therefore, the concept of fair trade has to do with the sustainability of trade and development in industrial economies as well as on the global level. Despite our rejection of criticism over globalization, here we have to point to the unfairness of trade that is felt on the side of industrial countries. It is the fact that inhuman exploration of resources in low-income countries may lead to price competition that cannot be followed by any economy following basic human rights and environmental principles. Here again, we come to a bend, where promoting fair trade is in the interest of industrial economies themselves.

In this respect, one should understand the rejection of globalism by numerous political leaders in the West. Not only are developed economies 'threatening' jobs in developed country, even the critics of Trade and Investment Partnership between the EU and USA partially point to the risk of losing jobs on both sides of Atlantic. Initiatives worrying about job preservation as, for instance, Campaign for America's future are quite specific about the risk of the TPP. In their communication from August 12, 2016, they line up behind the warning by former US presidency Democratic candidate Sanders, stating that '[*Obama administration*] continue pushing forward on the disastrous Trans-Pacific Partnership trade agreement that will cost American jobs, harm the environment, increase the cost of prescription drugs and threaten our ability to protect public health' [8]. The fact that this initiative considers itself as a fair trade movement only supports our above-presented perspective of a developed economy.

4. Globalization: from 'free trade' to 'fair trade'

Globalization stems from a basic human need to seek a better and more fulfilling life. Starting from such definition of globalization, we can say that it is the faithful companion of human's spiritual, economic and political development but also the expression of transportation and communication opportunities. Today globalization processes of the liberalization of the trade grew out of Bretton Woods Conference in 1944. After Bretton Woods Conference arose to establishing three important international institutions, in which the function is the foundation of the existence of relatively autonomous, state-regulated national economies, which to a limited extent set of meta-regulations: (1) the International Bank of Reconstruction and Development (IBRD, more commonly known as the World Bank); (2) the International Monetary Fund (IMF), the dollar-based gold exchange currency system; and (3) the General Agreement on Trade and Tariffs (GATT). These institutions proclaim and spread the 'free trade', 'free markets' and increasingly unrestricted access to a wide range of markets to transnational corporations.

As one of the child of this conference, the GATT came into existence in 1947 as part of a plan for general economic recovery after the Second World War. Then globalization discussions were carried out to remove the barriers to free trade under the GATT umbrella. The GATT's main purpose was to reduce barriers to international trade and it operated until 1994. Following the dissolution of the Cold War, the idea of globalization came to prominence, and in 1995 the GATT was replaced by the World Trade Organization (WTO). The WTO has promoted and developed the institutional foundations for 'free trade' as the important implications on the modes of production: free movement of goods and services together with the free movement of capital but not the free movement of labour.

Many authors locate globalization within economic phenomena and more specifically within the chain of production, trade and finance. As noted by Rosamond, '[f]or some, globalization simply refers to dramatically increased volumes in international trade. For others, globalization is better thought of as global economic integration, [...] cross-border flows of capital, goods, labour, and firms who creating genuinely global markets, which in turn accentuate the permeability of national economic borders' [9]. It is about the economistic definitions of

http://dx.doi.org/10.5772/66370

globalization and possibilities for economic governance. In a globalized world and transnational economic space, sovereign governments are losing the capacity to exercise effective economic governance over their own national jurisdictions, and their raison d'être becomes the adjustment of the domestic political economy to imperatives of powerful non-state forces that dominate the contemporary global economy.

The origin of the globalization movement was assumed to provide a framework for global equality and integration [10]. But very soon the globalization movement acquired a bad reputation: opposite globalization calls for a 'free trade' of goods and services has raised anti-globalism movement with the requirements of 'fair trade'. Stiglitz [11] argues that globalization could help to reduce poverty and serve both the developed and developing countries if approached with an appropriate attitude. He also believes that the main requirement for the success of globalization is the 'establishment of an equitable playing field'.

In the initial stages of globalization, multinational companies purchased their raw materials from any place in the world, wherever is the cheapest; conducted the production of goods and services in any country wherever it is cheapest (where the labour costs were the least), adding their brand and image to the product; and sold their goods and services in any country, in the markets where they can get the best price. Functioning of the mechanism of free trade has effectively increased global trade and global income.

But at the same time, globalization generated the painful consequences of exploitation of natural resources and abuses of labour in countries with lower production costs. The corporations of developed countries moved their production to the countries with abundant cheap labour; labourers of the developed countries started losing their jobs due to relocation in less-developed countries, increasing unemployment. All this leads to environmental degradation and growing inequalities in income distribution. These negative consequences, which were not consistent with the aspirations of people and society, have generated a strong desire for 'fair trade' in a global society. Direct results of globalization are such as to encourage the involvement in accordance with the same slogan: 'fair trade, not free trade' [12].

5. Governance: from abstraction to the lending criteria

Global finance markets and patterns of international trade in turn influence the shape of national economies. The contemporary rise of economic globalization has shifted attention from the role of government to the role of governance [13], and the globalization has fundamentally changed the context for governance.

Good governance is a fundamental ingredient of sustained economic development. But like 'fair trade', the term 'good governance' also is an abstraction that commands near-universal respect but diverse interpretation in myriad directions. The concept of good governance was defined by the requirements of a functioning market economy and institutional barriers to corruption, as a legitimate state with a democratic mandate, an efficient and open administration and the use of competition and markets in the public and private sectors. Good governance concerns an optimal division and interactions between government, market and civil society.

According to Bevir, 'governance refers to all processes of governing, whether undertaken by a government, market, or network; whether over a family, tribe, corporation, or territory; and whether by laws, norms, power, or language. Governance is a broader term than government because it focuses not only on the state and its institutions but also on the creation of rule and order in social practices' [14]. The governance describes changes in the nature and role of the state; it also denotes a programme for global reform—addressing poverty, gender equality, fair trade and sustainable environments. Governance expresses a widespread belief that the state increasingly depends on other organizations to secure its intentions, deliver its policies and establish a pattern of rule.

Various international agencies sought to specify the characteristics of good governance. It refers to the endeavour of international organizations (such as the United Nations, the World Bank, the IMF) to assess and measure the quality and stability of the governing institutions and practices, their transparency, responsiveness, procedural fairness, effectiveness, adherence to the rule of law, interaction, etc. The World Bank has defined good governance as 'the manner in which power is exercised in the management of a country's economic and social resources for development' [15]. Good governance is based on democratic values that stimulate administrative reforms that affect a range of organizations. A series of public-sector management reforms have been instituted on a global basis to improve the capacity of governments to respond to external demands for better and more responsive services, managing budget deficits and surpluses and addressing competitive pressures resulting from globalization. These ideas about the virtues of good governance became widespread and part of the everyday discourse of development practice. The United Nations' Commission on Human Rights [16] identifies transparency, responsibility, accountability, participation (inclusiveness) and responsiveness (to the needs of the people) as key attributes of good governance.

The growth of a set of global economic institutions (the IMF, the World Bank and the WTO) are held to be responsible for creating the formal rules and informal norms within which globalization is made possible. The World Bank [17] has compiled a list of six dimensions of public-sector governance that are used in an aggregate fashion to measure the quality of governance: voice and accountability, the rule of law, democratization, political stability and the absence of violence, government effectiveness and transparency, regulatory quality and control of corruption. Good governance is among the lending criteria used by the World Bank; it conceived of good governance primarily in terms of liberal democratic norms and practices (representative and responsible government, the rule of law, the absence of corruption) while also privileging a neoliberal faith in the superiority of market economies and the importance of introducing market mechanisms to the public sector.

As stated by Chhotray and Stocker [18], the criticism of good governance in development studies is set of power relations between North and South, and it fails to examine the construction of relationships in the context of structural inequality and disadvantage. 'Good governance principles are not adequate to the task of developmental imbalances, and as such, they are a smokescreen behind wider issues of fair trade, power redistribution, and social justice are hidden from view. It is rather to suggest that governance debates need to take place with due recognition given to the undermining effects of structural inequalities as a core part of the picture'.

Therefore, in the global governance, interactions occurring are private sustainability standard organizations who are regulating social and environmental standards in global production chains, for instance, in the forestry, tea, cocoa, coffee and apparel sectors. The private standard organizations set social and environmental standards across borders, in particular in global production chains that run from developing to developed countries [19]. As an outcome of global business governance, emerging are non-state certification programmes across policy sectors and industries in coffee production, forestry, fisheries, aquaculture, organic agriculture, etc. These programmes typically establish environmental performance standards and standards for socially responsible production with a fair wage and appropriate working condition. The demand for global market rules indeed comes from global corporations trying to create and stabilize regional or worldwide markets and thus can have an impact on public policies in the developed as well as the developing world. They go beyond voluntary codes of conduct and self-regulatory modes of governing, by requiring independent verification of compliance with standards and governance mechanisms. There are several standardization organizations and several types of fair trade standards, including standards for contract situations, for importers and also for the different products [20]. A fair trade certification is a product certification within the market-based movement fair trade. The most widely used fair trade certification is Fairtrade International (FLO), the International Fairtrade Certification Mark, used in Europe, Africa, Asia, Australia and New Zealand (equivalent standard in North American is Fair Trade Certification Mark).

6. What will bring us there?

Those are not only attempts to regulate international trade, who are bringing us in the direction of fair trade. Besides, international and regional trade agreements are positioning one specific region in front of the others and can therefore not be seen as a progress in sense of fair sustainable trade.

Individual, academic and NGO endeavours surely have a positive impact on fair trade and are acting practically in the same direction. When ability to act is in question, one should beware the crucial difference between the actors listed above and governments. As stated above, there are not just the commitments of industrial countries' governments to regulate international trade, which lead to fair sustainable trade, but the typical concern and pressure of Western powers in the sense of human rights and democratization. Democratization presents, in addition to social and economic development, the other great driving force for changes in the world. Although in 1974 less than three in ten nations in the world could be classified as democratic, 20 years later in 1994, that number had grown to six in ten, and at the beginning of the twenty-first century, most of these newly established democracies have survived and joined by a few more recruits [21]. But it is not just the spread of the basic institutions of liberal democracy, but rather that the idea of democracy has gained a certain universal appeal. The rise of democracy requires space for governance and lays out conditions for governance practice.

As stated above, globalization is often treated as a peril of modern times. We accept Stiglitz's view that pro-globalization policy should be undertaken properly and consider the historical and cultural experience of the individual country [11]. On the other side, we believe that this responsibility cannot simply be assigned to the party assuring the resources in this process. It is probably not the responsibility of international organizations to study in depth the whole bunch of historical and cultural developments, which had led to a country's present economic perils (especially the IMF). Financial support means money and the money means trust. To assure the trust, local governments have to be ready to abolish main practices that led to the problem. Since here are mostly traditional societies, this is almost impossible to achieve without changing governance approach, which quickly can lead to a restructuring of power. Not ready for accepting these risks, governments in countries subject to economic help prefer to accept the arrangements and criticize them later.

If we can put aside the above stressed negative impact of globalization, we could again argue that it rather brings problems to industrial countries. As a principle due to the free movement of capital, it should technically bring advantage to low-income economies with abundant labour force—especially if it is educated enough. As stated above, from the trade perspective, it enables them to fill the gaps in products and services where up to now development in industrial countries has led to rights and privileges (costs) that are unsustainable from the theoretical perspective of the law of one price.

Due to the transparency globalization brings, it should rather be treated as a factor of fair sustainable trade. Therefore, we agree to the statements of authors as is Bhagwati [22] pointing that 'globalization has a human face and that it advances, rather than inhibits, the achievement of social agendas as wide-ranging as the promotion of gender equality worldwide and the reduction of poverty and child labour in poor countries'.

Typically, American political parties have different views on trade positions, where the Democratic Party is the only one touching this phenomenon. The Liberal Party opposes any agreement and regulation, while the Republican Party presents rather mercantilist views ('U.S. should position itself to dominate trade, promote free trade with America setting the standards'). The Democratic Party platform on Free trade [23] shows more understanding of the whole issue. Unlike above-presented definitions, this platform uses the only explicable platform of 'knocking down barriers to free, balanced and fair trade'.

If we try to assess the recent developments of fair trade initiatives, we see that eventually they meet economics of scale issues, and it is the question how to keep business technology change outside producers included in a traditional fair trade. Growing into a supranational organization, Fairtrade International (FLO) is demonstrating a typical risk of megastructures—here meaning, for instance, arguments over logo going on between FLO and their sister organization Equal Exchange [24]. By opposing the inclusion of plantation production, it is excluding those who work there and live from it, which means neglecting the population making their

http://dx.doi.org/10.5772/66370

living in organization forms established prior to emerging of fair trade initiatives. On the other hand, it is clear that individual producers will eventually have to be included in some kind of cooperative production due to the requirements of economic of scale and modern business technologies. At the end of the day to be competitive, the webs of producer and cooperatives will have to show its ability to include a broad band of the stakeholders in the governance, policy development and ownership.

Typical requirements of the USA, EU and allies in their geopolitical positions refer to human rights. Typically, their involvement up to now has shown that they lack information and patience to realize this basic principle in traditional countries without turmoil. But one should understand that disequilibria in global trade have to do a lot with inappropriate personal treatment and dignity in traditional societies [25]. The perspective of the fair trade initiative, therefore, is close related to the human rights. There are several efficient individual and NGO's initiatives that strive for inclusion of human rights principles into daily policy, but it is clear that it will be the western governments' achievements that human rights are put onto agenda of most influential global summits that will decisively boost fair trade development.

7. Conclusions

Transparency, accountability, governance and democratization have therefore a lot to do with fair trade. They seem quite indirect facts but can only be basic principles for the fair trade. Therefore, direct individual actions to achieve fair trade (will always) have only limited effect. Let us finish with the provocative statement that will hardly be accepted by most of the readership: rather than through trivial action in the form of well-minded historical anthropomorphism, we will achieve more with democratic pressures on the global aspect of the international policy of most powerful governments of industrial countries.

The action of governments of developed countries should base on two pillars. The first pillar is the knowledge and understanding of historical and cultural fundament of developments in low-income countries. The second one is patient policy and acting. This means abolishment of biased support of groups prone to swift action. Up to now such policy did not bring anything else than an acceleration of existing problems and discrepancies.

There are not only governments of influential economies but also financial international organizations that can support the idea of fair trade. IMF and World Bank are here to step into support adjustment of local producers for international standards and competition. This will have to be trimmed to seek for domestic government's support for institutional adjustment which is a project far exceeding the possible outcome of direct fair trade initiatives.

The strongest impediment to fair trade development now is the mistrust between biggest economies. Although China points to their trade reforms bringing in reciprocity [26], the Trump programme forms their position basing on allegations that China manipulates its currency to retain its competitiveness, ignoring intellectual property laws, and is exercising illegal export subsidies [27]. In this respect, German government shows more readiness to accept the principles of fair sustainable trade by reducing agricultural subsidies and abolishing export subsidies, opening up markets in industrialized countries and promoting fair terms and conditions of employment [28]. These surely are not circumstances where most influential world governments could pursue fair trade policy, which is the only solution for assuring sustainable economic developments and sustainability.

What will probably happen? One could only hope that the time when nationalist parties gain on territory will end and that the cost of their action will not be too high. We will realize that we risk too much with building walls. This is against the impact that technology change has on business and society. Then it will be natural to strive for greater cooperation on sustainable principles. From the point of the theory of economic policy, the cooperation and inclusion are the basic argument why we need a system, e.g., institutional setting in a national economy. Its role is to assure the cooperation between economic agents. As a public good, it can only be offered by the government—in this specific case driven by economic principles and democratic pressure.

Acknowledgements

We would like to thank Petra Cajnko, who helped with the literature in the starting phase of this study.

Author details

Rasto Ovin* and Pedja Ašanin Gole

*Address all correspondence to: rasto.ovin@doba.si

DOBA Business School, Maribor, Slovenia

References

[1] Norman, L. (2016) 'Growing Percentage of People Arriving in EU Are Economic Migrants, Commission Says. Jan. 26, 2016', *The Wall Street Journal*. Available at: http://www.wsj.com/articles/growing-percentage-of-people-arriving-in-eu-are-economic-migrants-commission-says-1453815921 [16.8.2016].

[2] *See:* FINE (2001) *Fair Trade Definition and Principles*. Brussels: Fair Trade Advocacy Office.

[3] WFTO (2014) *Defining Fair Trade*. Available at: http://www.wfto.com/about-us/history-wfto [28.7.2016]

[4] Bevir, M. (ed.) (2010) *Encyclopedia of Political Theory*. Thousand Oaks, London, New Delhi, Singapore: SAGE Publications, p. 491.

[5] Fairtrade Foundation (2016) *What is Fairtrade?*. Available at: http://www.fairtrade.org.uk/en/what-is-fairtrade [9.8.2016].

[6] *cf.* Harrison, B., Harris, J. and Deardorff, M. (2014) *American Democracy Now*. 4th ed. New York: McGraw-Hill Education.

[7] Ritzer, G. (2011) Globalization: The Essentials. Malden, Oxford, West Sussex: Wiley Blackwell, A John Wiley & Sons, pp. 295–297

[8] Johnson, D. (2016) 'President Tells Congress TPP Is Coming Their Way. What Will Clinton Do?', *OurFuture.org*, 12 August. Available at: https://ourfuture.org/20160812/president-notifies-congress-tpp-is-coming-their-way [17.8.2016].

[9] Rosamond, B. (2007) 'Economic Governance', in Bevir, M. (ed.) *Encyclopedia of Governance*. Thousand Oaks, London, New Delhi: SAGE Publications, pp. 350–353.

[10] Stiglitz, J.E. (2003) 'We Have to Make Globalization Work for All: Reforms of the Trade and Financial Systems are Imperative', *YaleGlobal Online*. Available at: http://yaleglobal.yale.edu/content/we-have-make-globalization-work-all [17.8.2016].

[11] Stiglitz, J.E. (2002) *Globalization and Its Discontents*. New York: W.W. Norton & Company.

[12] *cf.* Crowther, D. and Aras, G. (2010) 'Overview: Globalisation and Corporate Governance', in Aras, G. and Crowther, D. (ed.) *A Handbook of Corporate Governance and Social Responsibility*. Farnham and Burlington: Gower Publishing Limited, pp. 1–4, *and* Ritzer, 2011.

[13] Jessop, B. (1995) 'The Regulation Approach, Governance and Post-Fordism: Alternative Perspectives on Economic Change?', *Economy and Society*, 24, pp. 307–333.

[14] Ansell, C. and Bevir, M. (ed.) (2013) *A Theory of Governance*. Berkeley, Los Angeles, London: University of California Press, p. 1.

[15] The World Bank (1992) *Governance and Development*. Washington, DC: The World Bank. Available at: http://documents.worldbank.org/curated/en/604951468739447676/Governance-and-development [6.9.2014], p. 1.

[16] United Nations' Commission on Human Rights (2016) *Good Governance and Human Rights*. Available at: http://www.ohchr.org/EN/Issues/Development/GoodGovernance/Pages/Good GovernanceIndex. aspx [8.8.2016].

[17] *cf.* Williams, D. and Young, T. (1994) 'Governance, the World Bank, and Liberal Theory', *Political Studies*, 75, pp. 84–100.

[18] Chhotray, V. and Stoker, G. (2009) *Governance Theory and Practice: A Cross-Disciplinary Approach*. Basingstoke: Palgrave Macmillan, p. 222.

[19] Fransen, L. (2015) 'The Politics of Meta-Governance in Transnational Private Sustainability Governance', *Policy Science*. USA: Springer, 48, pp. 293–317. doi: 10.1007/s11077-015-9219-8, pp. 293–296.

[20] *cf.* Smelser, N.J. and Swedberg, R. (ed.) (2005) *The Handbook of Economic Sociology*. 2nd ed. Princeton, Oxford, New York: Princeton University Press, Russell Sage Foundation.

[21] Diamond, L. (2003) 'Universal Democracy?', *Policy Review*, 119(June/July), pp. 3–25. Available at: http://cddrl.stanford.edu/publications/universal_democracy [18.3.2012].

[22] Bhagwati, J.N. (2004) *What Enriches The Poor And Liberates The Oppressed?, Council on Foreign Relations*. Available at: http://www.cfr.org/globalization/enriches-poor-liberates-oppressed/p6843 [4.8.2016].

[23] On the issues (2016) *American Parties on Free Trade*. Available at: http://www.ontheissues.org/Celeb/Democratic_Party_Free_Trade.htm [17.8.2016].

[24] Gunther, M. (2012) *The Schism Over Fair Trade*. Available at: www.marcgunther.com/a-schism-over-trade [17.8.2016].

[25] Fitzgerald, C.S. (2009) '*Toward A Central American Fair Trade Agreement*', Advocates' Forum: University of Chicago School of Social Service Administration. Available at: https://ssa.uchicago.edu/toward-central-american-fair-trade-agreement [8.8.2016].

[26] Embassy of the Republic of China in the United States of America (2007) *China's Foreign Trade*. Available at: http://www.china-embassy.org/eng/zt/bps/t943740.htm [6.8.2016].

[27] Trump Pence Make America Great Again (2016) *Reforming the U.S Trade Relationship to Make America Great Again*. Available at: https://www.donaldjtrump.com/positions/us-china-trade-reform [11.8.2016].

[28] Federal Ministry for Economic Cooperation and Development (2016) *What Germany Is Doing: Fair Rules in International Trade*. Available at: http://www.bmz.de/en/what_we_do/issues/wirtschaft/welthandel/deutsches_engagement/index.html [9.8.2016].

Chapter 3

Risks Associated with International Trading of Medicines by Non-Licensed Entities and Non-Professionals

Ntambwe Malangu

Additional information is available at the end of the chapter

http://dx.doi.org/10.5772/66471

Abstract

The making, distribution and trading of medicines can be traced back as far as antiquity. When talking about trading, sale or dispensing of medicines, it is almost impossible to separate this topic with the profession of pharmacy or pharmacists. Although most countries introduced legislations that put the trading of medicines largely in the hand of licensed businesses and professionals mainly pharmacists, informal and international trading of medicines and related substances has continued to be practiced in almost all countries due to loopholes in legislations among other reasons. This chapter highlights the risks associated with the trading of medicines by unlicensed organisations and non-professionals. These risks include the production and sale of counterfeit medicines, encouraging abuse and misuse of medicines, anti-competitive behaviour and so on. The major findings are that concessions made to allow non-licensed businesses and non-professionals to trade in medicines have resulted in several consequences that are threatening the whole world. It is this realisation that has prompted the recommendation that courage from decision makers is required for them to take a stand and hand over back the trading of medicines firmly in the hands of licensed professionals while outlawing loopholes that sustained the trade of medicines by unlicensed entities and non-professionals.

Keywords: informal, illegal, trade, medicines, non-licensed, non-professional

1. Introduction

The making, distribution and trading of medicines can be traced back as far as antiquity. The making, production or manufacturing of medicines, mixtures, admixtures and other dosages forms have been performed over the years by a wide categories of people including lay people, priests, herbalists, traditional healers, midwives, medical doctors, nurses and pharmacists. As elaborated below, the practice of the art of healing was based on Arab, Egyptian, Greek and Roman texts, particularly those of Hippocrates, Aristotle, Dioscorides, Galen and others. The making of medicines was the domain of monasteries and local healers as medical training was not formalised then. The formal training and development of preparation techniques of medicinal mixtures based on standardised processes of harvesting, drying and distillation led to the abandonment of the old-fashioned herbal preparations practices by lay people who fell out of favour with the professionalization of the healing/medical community. But the distribution, sale as well as the local and international trade of medicines have been performed, in addition, by licensed and non-licensed people and businesses. This paper aims to describe and report on the risks associated with the trading of medicines by non-licensed business entities and non-professionals. In doing so, the paper elaborates on the reasons why international trade is prone to being conducted by unlicensed businesses and non-professionals, as well as on the sources of medicines traded.

In order to accomplish the above, the literature search, without any date limitation, was conducted to retrieve and include relevant articles published in English. The key words used were as follows: drugs, medicines, trading, illegal, informal, unlicensed and non-professionals. In the following pages, a brief overview on the historical perspective of the trading of medicines as a profession is presented. It is followed by a section elaborating on the trading of medicines by non-licensed and non-professionals. The remainder of the chapter is about issues specifically addressing the objectives of the paper as described above.

2. Trading of medicines as a profession

When talking about trading, sale or dispensing of medicines, it is almost impossible to separate this topic with the profession of pharmacy or pharmacists. From written history, it is established that the making, storing, supplying, issuing or selling and administration of medicines has been the prerogatives of people with combined skills of priest, physician and pharmacist. Earliest known prescriptions by Egyptians date as far back as 2700 B.C; documents such as the medical papyri of Kahun and Ramesseum [about 2040 B.C], the Edwin Smith and Hearst Papyri, the Lesser Berlin Papyrus [which dated from about 1600 B.C] and the Ebers Papyrus [about 1552 B.C] refer to medicines. On the Ebers Papyrus, there is a record of a formulary that listed about 700 medicines together with instructions on their compounding. Some of these medicines are still used today as excipients, adjuvants, solvents or active ingredients, such as alcohol [wines], acetic acid [vinegar], castor oil, myrrh, wormwood, aloes, magnesia, opium [source of narcotic compounds], peppermint, psyllium (Metamuci®) and many others [1, 2].

Similarly, the Chinese pharmacy (about 2000 BC)] as practiced by the Emperor Shen Nung who wrote the Pen Tsao or great/natural herbal, a manuscript that enumerated 350 medicinal entities with a distinction made about what is to be used by physicians and another for pharmacists. This is one of the old documents expressing the separation of duties between medical doctors and pharmacists long before the Palermo edit as explained below. With the constant change of balance of military conquests that saw alternative dominances and colonization between African and European empires between the first and the seventh century AD, the Greek having gained the upper hand, their writings provide some more clarity on the practice of pharmacy [1–3].

During the first century AD, in his *Materia Medica,* Dioscorides listed 500 remedies prepared from plants, animals and metals. During the second century AD, it is Galen (130–201) who devised a system of pathology and therapy that ruled western medicine for over a thousand years. He wrote a compendium describing the preparation of medicines, thus earning himself the title of the "father of pharmacy" [3].

It should be noted also that the Arab physician, Rhazes (865–925 AD), wrote, in his "*Liber Continens,*" some of basic principles of pharmacotherapy such as "if you can heal with foods, then do no prescribe medicines." Later on, Dr. Ali ibn Sina (980–1037 AD) wrote a medical reference book, "Canon Medicinae" that summarised and expanded on principles of therapeutics and pharmacotherapy that have been influential from sixteenth to twentieth centuries [1–5].

It should be stated that throughout Europe, the roles of the physician, pharmacist and priest were intertwined. This threesome combination was and is still illustrative of the roles of custodians of medicines; namely, being able to determine what is wrong with a person; knowing what products should be used to treat what is wrong; and being compassionate for the well-being of the person with no financial incentive as primary consideration. It is the German Emperor Frederick II who, in 1231 AD, issued an edict known as the "Palermo Edict". This legal document entrenched the separation of the practices of medicine and pharmacy, giving rise to the profession of pharmacy in Europe. In addition, this edict made provision for the official supervision of pharmacy practice and instructed pharmacists to prepare quality drugs according to their skilled art, in a consistent and standardised manner. This proclamation was followed by similar legislations in other parts of Europe; by 1408, the first Poison Acts was passed in Scotland by order of James I [1, 2, 6].

As Europeans explored the world, the Portuguese, Dutch and English navigators opened sea routes around the world with increased trading of diverse goods. By the fifteenth century, the trade in medicinal plants, health products and spices was a lucrative business that led to many conflicts between the Spanish, the Portuguese, the Dutch, the French and the British in their efforts to control the sources of these prized commodities [7, 8]. By the sixteenth century when Africa was finally made submissive, the ensuing massive slave trade went along with the demise of pharmacy in Africa but a growth of pharmacists as professionals in Europe and America [9–12]. As such, pharmacists known then as 'apothecaries of the company of Grocers' held the skills and knowledge on the preparations of concoctions, potions and other dosages forms due to several innovations as explained below [3, 13].

One major element of that growth was the production of reference books that became widespread occurrence after the invention of printing in Europe. The first attempt to standardisation was made in Florence [Italy] where the first official pharmacopoeia the "Ricettario Florentino" was produced in 1498, and a few years later was translated into Latin so that it could be used throughout Europe. The City of Nuremburg in 1529 was the first community to use a formulary legally binding on all apothecaries of that city [3, 14, 15].

Hence, during the sixteenth and seventieth centuries, the art of the apothecary was developing rapidly in Europe such that in 1617, King James 1st of England granted the Apothecaries a royal charter which separated them from the Grocers. It is reported that the Grocers tried to resist, but the King stood firm as he saw the grocers as merchants having no professional skill, whilst the practice of the apothecary was an art practiced with skill and knowledge. By 1815, the Apothecaries Act of 1815 was passed. The net impact of the new Apothecaries Act was a clearer definition of the two professions, medicine and pharmacy [2, 3, 16–18].

3. Trading of medicines by non-licensed entities and non-professionals

The above brief historic overview served to show that the business of trading in medicines was largely into the hands of professionals. However, with the colonization of Africa, the loss of its manpower through slavery, the plundering of its resources and the demise of its major centres of learning in Egypt, Mali and other parts of the continent, the professionalization of pharmacy in Africa lagged behind in comparison to Europe, Asia and America [6, 19–21].

As illustrated above from the history of pharmacy in England, most European countries enacted legislation to place the trade of medicines in the hand of pharmacists and medical doctors; though informal trading continued unabated due to the lucrative nature of the trade, the loopholes in legislations and the recognition that herbal medicine practice was vested with some people through heredity and initiation but not academic training [22–25].

Nowadays, in Africa and South America, fraudsters posing as genuine traditional healers have exploited again the lack of regulation of traditional and herbal medicine practices to enter in disguise into informal trade of conventional medicines. They often buy medicines from legitimate outlets and repackage them and sell them [26, 27].

Moreover, the grocers and small traders of basic necessity goods are still the most common business entities from which people procure most household items including medicines for minor ailments. This situation results from regulatory concessions based on the classification of medicines in categories taking into account the probabilities of harm; with grocers being authorized to sell medicines deemed less harmful or over-the-counter drugs [27–30].

Hence, in Denmark, South Africa and several other countries, for instance, shops outside the pharmacy sector are allowed to or in some instances can obtain authorisation to sell over-the-counter (OTC) medicines that are suitable for sale outside pharmacies. In Denmark, it is the Danish Medicines Agency which decides whether a medicine can be sold at these shops; in South Africa, the Medicines Council establishes the list of Unscheduled Medicines suitable for sale outside licensed pharmacies. The staff employed at shops outside the pharmacy sector are not required to have a pharmaceutical education. The general mercantile shops are required to keep and sell OTCs as defined by the Danish Medicines Agency or the South African Medicines Council. These OTCs include products such as painkillers, cough suppressants, lozenges for a sore throat as well as nicotine chewing gums and some other remedies for the digestive system [31–34].

In Africa and South America, where most legislations were inherited from countries that colonised them, several countries had regulations on pharmacy similar to the ones of European countries. After independence, several countries continued to implement the Poisons Act or Pharmacy Act or Medicines Act until 1980s–1990s. It is during this period that several countries with the help of the World Health Organisation revised, updated or developed their pharmaceutical policies, regulations on registrations and sale of medicines, and the exercise of the pharmacy profession [35–40].

With the practice of traditional medicine well entrenched in Africa and Asia, the opportunities brought by the ease of packaging and transportation led to an ever-existing informal sale of medicinal plants, herbal and conventional medicines. Because the loopholes inherited from colonial laws still persists, informal trade of medicines and medicinal herbs on the streets and in non-licensed businesses is still a common sight in most African and other developing countries [41–44].

The practice known as informal trading or selling of medicines by unlicensed people and businesses is a widespread phenomenon facilitated by the lack of effective legislation, regulations and enforcement thereof. The international trade of drugs, medicines, chemicals and cosmetics both legitimate and grey markets have been and still is fuelled by financial gains. One of the underlying factors is the non-existing of formal trading outlets in some areas, particularly in urban slums and rural areas of most developing countries. During the end of twentieth century, unemployment has been also a driving force in the proliferation of informal trade of medicines; other factors will be discussed further [45–48].

The hallmarks of informal health products traders are that they have not been trained in pharmacy or any health-related professions and are not registered with any professional councils or regulatory bodies. Consequently, they are free agents whose sole motive to trade in medicines is to make money. Moreover, since the start of industrialisation in Europe, the subsequent decline in the formulation and preparation of medicines in community pharmacy outlets led to the transfer of the production or manufacturing of medicines in the hands of business entities owned by non-professionals or businessmen. As explained below, with the profit motive as primary consideration, this control of production and distribution of medicines by non-professionals has and still is a facilitating factor for the trading of medicines by non-professionals on the streets through the channels as explained below [49–50].

These businesses may be properly licensed to trade in medicines or cosmetics or other products; some may not be licensed but exploit loopholes in legislations to trade in medicines such as subcontracting companies and more recently as internet-based companies that are selling medicines. The characteristics of non-licensed entities are that they are not registered with regulatory bodies in the countries from which they operate, they are not run by professionals, and thus have no professional ethical allegiance. Like individuals, the sole purpose of these businesses is to make money from selling or trading health commodities and medicines without any consideration for the well-being of the people they sell their products to [51–54].

4. Why international trade of medicines is prone to illicit and unprofessional practices

The lack of professional ethics, compassion and concern for others is one of several considerations rendering international trade of medicines prone to illegal, illicit and unprofessional practices. Chief among the reasons is that fact that some countries, even, those with stringent medicines regulatory authority and control infrastructure, have legislated that medicines destined for export need not conform to legal requirements and standards laid down for medicines destined for their national or local consumption [55–58]. This discriminatory legislation which essentially tells manufacturers that their products that do not meet national standards should be exported is in itself one of the sources of substandard medicines that are flooding international trade. Indeed, when manufacturers know well that their products cannot be sold locally or exported to countries with strong quality control system, they will find unguarded outlets to do so [43, 59–61].

Parallel trade, a legitimate operation as explained below is often implicated as a potential way for illicit and unscrupulous counterfeiters to infiltrate the legitimate supply of medications as the medicines move between wholesalers and distributors after manufacturing and before reaching the last mile, or facilities dealing directly with end-users such as retail pharmacies, clinics and hospitals. Because of price differentiation based on the type of market, products available more cheaply in one market can be sold legally in another market at a higher price [36, 40, 45, 51, 62–64].

Hence, as medicines are shifted from market to market or more precisely from country to country, the original packaging and inserts in one language are replaced and repackaged with new ones in another desired language; in the process anti-counterfeiting features, such as holograms, are discarded entirely and legally so [57, 63, 64]. Worse, if the original packaging is not destroyed, it may be picked up by counterfeiters from landfills and reused. Thus, even countries with strong regulatory quality assurance system will be pried on this way as many legitimate pharmaceutical entities use parallel trade.

Parallel trading has been implicated also in the trading of counterfeit drugs. Several versions of fake Coartem®, an antimalaria product have been found in many African cities. Some seemed to have been manufactured for the African market as its packaging carried the logo of Nigeria's medicines regulator, the National Agency for Food and Drug Administration and Control—which is used as a seal of approval for authentic Coartem® throughout the continent. However, small details could have been noticed by a trained eye (**Figure 1**), in that the fake Coartem® in all three countries had an expiry date of 24 months instead of the usual 23 months for genuine Coartem®; some products had several languages errors; other versions had incorrect number of tablets in them [57, 65–69].

The above situation illustrates the consequences of the lack of oversight of the medicines supply chain by professionals such as pharmacists. This is why it is still another failure when some countries allow wholesalers that are not subjected to their pharmaceutical legislation such as general merchants, to import non-prescriptions drugs. These businesses that operate without professional oversight by pharmacists may also fall prey to international criminal syndicates that may use their operations to add to their consignments other products including counterfeit drugs as explained above [59, 60]. Moreover, the weak capacity in developing countries at customs and the fact that the bribing of officials ensures that any consignment can enter a country facilitates the illicit trade [70].

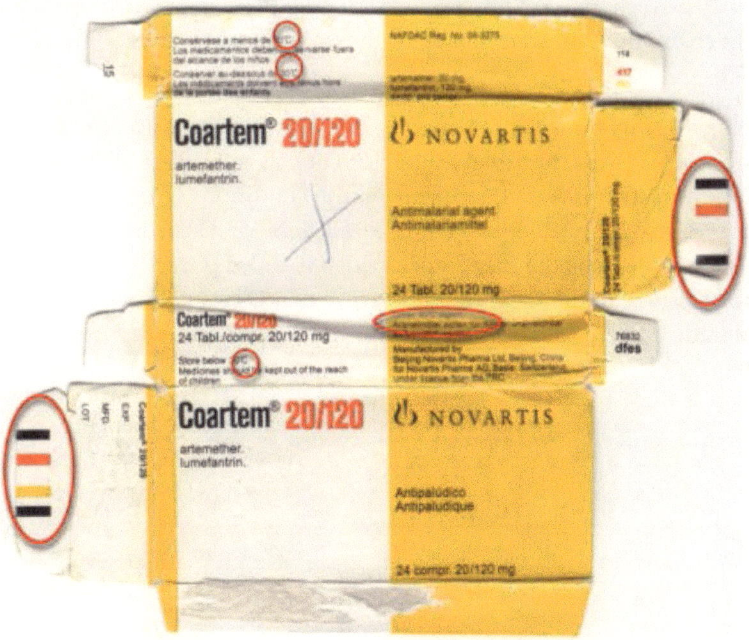

Figure 1. Features differentiating fake and genuine Coartem®. Source: Newton et al. [56].

Most importantly, weak legislations and penalties facilitate illicit trade in medicines and counterfeit medicines. For instance, the penalty for manufacturing or distributing counterfeit drugs is very lenient in many countries. It is noteworthy that about 10 years ago, in Nigeria, a person convicted for such an offense faced an imprisonment periods ranging between 3 months and 5 years or had an option of paying a fine of 70–3600 US dollars. Similarly in some South American countries, the penalty for illicit trade or in drug counterfeiting was no more than six months in jail or an option to pay a fine [49–60, 62, 71-72].

The advent of internet-based businesses that cannot be inspected by pharmaceutical inspectors because of lack of physical storage facilities within the same location as the registered address of the business, the ease of reproducing original documents due to improved printing technology and the lack of quality assurance skills and systems in several developing countries, constitute some of the other factors that encourages the illegal international trade of medicines as well as the unfortunate existence of unscrupulous manufacturers and criminal syndicates [73–77].

5. Sources of medicines traded by unlicensed entities and non-professionals

Conceptually, at the core, medicines sold by unlicensed entities and non-professionals originate from either legitimate manufacturers or unlicensed, underground manufacturers (**Figure 2**). Legitimate manufacturers typically sell their products directly to primary wholesalers who will then sell to secondary even tertiary wholesalers depending on the architecture of the supply chain, the countries involved, the volume or quantities and types of products traded [51, 73].

As explained above, wholesalers may legally sell the OTC products to unlicensed retailers. From this point, unlicensed, informal traders can buy as much OTC products from the retailers due to lack of restrictions on quantities, on the conditions of transport or distribution of the products and most importantly, the non-application of restricting or controlling pharmaceutical regulations such as the mandatory registers to keep track of who bought what and how much. This is one of the most common ways that OTC and prescription products enter the informal trade and are sold on the streets of most developing countries [78, 79].

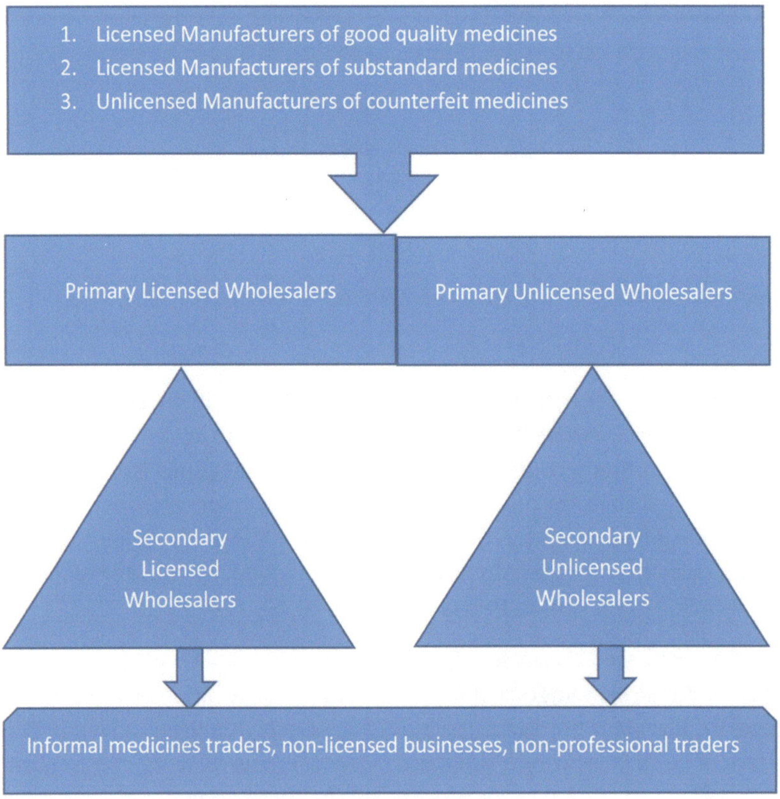

Figure 2. Sources of medicines traded by non-licensed businesses and non-professionals. Source: Author's illustration.

http://dx.doi.org/10.5772/66471

In the same vein, some unscrupulous legitimate manufacturers may knowingly sell their substandard products to primary or secondary wholesalers and even directly to retailers of countries with little or no established or well-performing quality assurance systems and through collusion or fraudulent practices get the products to informal traders who will then get hold of these products and sell them on the streets. Since informal traders have no means, knowledge or even interest in ascertaining the quality of the products they sell, this avenue gives unscrupulous licensed manufacturers to trade or get rid of their substandard products [41, 48–51].

As illustrated above, it goes without saying that unlicensed or underground manufacturers will use their primary unlicensed wholesalers to sale their substandard products or most commonly their counterfeit products. These products usually continue in the illegal, informal, criminal and fraudulent routes throughout until they reach the street vendors. It has been documented that counterfeit products may also enter the legitimate routes through corruption, collusion and fraud as explained below.

Basically, the entities involved may be a mix of legitimate and unlicensed entities as well as corrupt customs officials. In this collaboration of wrongdoers, consignments of the substandard and counterfeit products get included into legitimate purchases [59–60, 64, 70, 74]. This may be achieved by simply reproducing the legitimate documents and adding a "zero" to the original quantities ordered, and then supplying the difference. For instance, a legitimate primary wholesaler of a country A may have ordered 9000 Bottles of Aspirin 300 mg pack of 1000 tablets. The fraudsters will change the quantities to 90,000 × 1000 Bottles of Aspirin 300 mg, so they will add to such a consignment 81,000 bottles of 1000 tablets of Aspirin.

With corrupt officials at countries' borders and the collusion with the primary wholesalers who initiated the purchase orders, the products will enter a country even if they were prohibited, or controlled drugs due to the absence of rigorous controls. As explained above during the procedures carried out as part of parallel trade, changes in packaging, relabelling and reconditioning provide opportunities for falsifying and counterfeiting even legitimate products [45, 62–65, 80–82].

Other sources of medicines sold by unlicensed entities are the stealing of legitimate shipments destined to wholesalers or retailers. This happens at seas or during road transport. Products from theft are generally genuine and of good quality at the time of their acquisition. However, due to incorrect storage, inadequate handling and improper transportation, their quality may deteriorate rapidly to the extent that by the time they reach the street vendors, they are already as good as impotent products. Several studies have reported how heat-sensitive medicines, notably, vaccines, antibiotics and anti-malaria products have been transported and stored in inappropriate conditions leading them to degrade [62, 66, 83, 84].

In some instances, travellers have been arrested for having smuggled in their luggage, prescription drugs destined for illegal and informal trade (see insert photo above, **Figure 3**). In other instances, qualified doctors have been forced to write prescriptions under coercion for controlled drugs that the criminals fill at the pharmacies and sell on the streets. Moreover, stealing also can be organised by criminals who approach healthcare professionals working in hospitals pharmacies and other pharmaceutical outlets and thus obtain legitimate products that are subsequently sold to consumers through illegal and unlicensed businesses and outlets. It should be noted that non-professional healthcare workers or support staff members have been and are also a source of stolen products from health facilities. These products end up in the streets to be sold by unlicensed entities and non-professionals including legitimate or illegitimate traditional healers, herbalists, drug dispensers and other small traders [85–89].

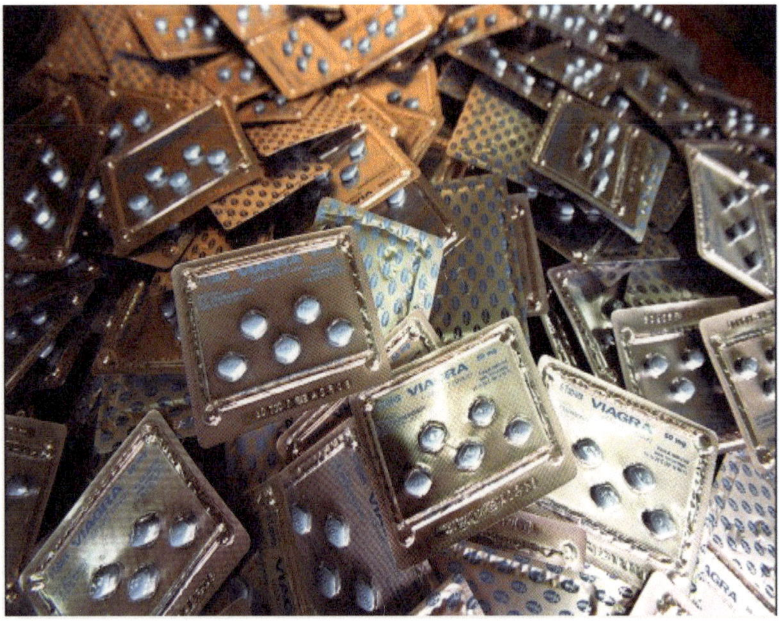

Figure 3. Viagra® bust by South African customs officials worth ZAR 40 million [about 2.8 million USD] Photo: Patrick Aventurier/Gamma-Rapho via Getty Images. Source: https://www.enca.com/south-africa/sars-biggest-viagra-bust.

6. Risk associated with the trading of medicines by non-licensed entities and non-professionals

As explained above, the rationale trading in medicines by non-licensed businesses and non-professionals is to make a living, make money or make a profit from the legal or illegal sale of medicines. Indeed, as alluded to, some entities maybe licensed to sale legally medicines as in Denmark, South Africa and other countries. Due to the lack of a requirement for these businesses to record the transactions of medicines, a client may go through several grocery shops and procure as many painkillers or sleeping tablets for instance and get enough to use for suicide or to intoxicate their unsuspecting victims [30–33, 90]. The above illustrate the ever-present risk of the handling of small quantities of medicines by non-professionals. Several other risks exist as detailed below.

http://dx.doi.org/10.5772/66471

6.1. Criminality

6.1.1. Acute criminal poisoning

Several instances of acute poisoning have been reported as resulting from pharmaceutical products that have been disposed of unconventionally and irresponsibly by unlicensed entities and non-professionals. Most importantly, pharmaceutical, agro-chemicals and other products that have been involved in acute deliberate poisoning whether for suicide, parasuicide or with criminal intent have been acquired from the unlicensed street vendors [91, 92]. As explained above informal trading of medicines online or street-vending is unrestricted, uncontrolled and based on the sole purpose for the vendors to make quick money. Hence, even children may purchase these products indiscriminately. Other studies have reported underage patients having purchased prohibited substances including medicines and other substances from online, streets and from non-professional traders in Africa, Asia, Europe and elsewhere [90, 93–97].

6.1.2. Production and distribution of substandard and counterfeit drugs

As reported above, one of the major risks of unlicensed trading of medicines is that it fuels the criminal production and distribution of substandard, falsified and counterfeit medicines by criminal syndicates that operate in several countries. The World Health Organization (WHO) has defined counterfeit medications as products that are deliberately and fraudulently mislabelled with respect to identity and or source. The act of counterfeiting applies to products whether there are branded and generics; counterfeit products include products with the correct ingredients in insufficient dosing or quantity or quality; or with the wrong ingredient with/without active ingredients in insufficient amount or too much of it; or with products with fake packaging similar to the original product packaging. Furthermore, these products may often contain unlicensed analogues or mixtures of active ingredients that have not been evaluated for efficacy and safety in clinical trials; furthermore, their toxicity, pharmacokinetic, pharmacodynamics and drug interaction profiles have not been established [62, 63, 67, 98, 99].

The scale of the production is now a major concern to the international community because the proceeds of the sale of these medicines may be being used to finance other criminal activities including terrorism. It is estimated that illegal trading of drugs may have generated US $531.6 billion in 2013 [100]. The range of counterfeit products reaching markets is broad including fast-moving OTCs, generics as well-branded high-tech products. It is estimated that in more than 50% of cases, medicines purchased over the internet from illegal sites that conceal their physical address have been found to be counterfeits [101]. The type of counterfeit drugs most frequently faked in developing countries are medicines used for infectious diseases such as antibiotics and anti-malarial products. Counterfeit antimalarial drugs are widespread in developing countries, particularly Southeast Asia and Africa; hence, even fake antiretroviral drugs have been reported in Africa. In developed countries, drugs used for chronic conditions such as anticancer, lipid lowering drugs, anti-allergic, endocrine agents (both hormones and steroids), as well as drugs for the erectile dysfunction predominate. With regard to Viagra®, results from analysis of recovered samples showed that only 14% of the samples had been authentic; and of the 626 UK samples, 83% of these samples were counterfeit [102–109].

6.2. Price increase and unfair competition

The sale of medicines by unlicensed vendors results in several anti-competitive behaviours. On one hand, for most prescription drugs, the prices of these drugs sold on the streets at less than half their normal prices. This is the chief reason that pushes consumers to buy these products as they believe to be saving money by buying from the streets in comparison to how much they would have paid from pharmacies. It is well-established that substandard products are generally cheaper than genuine products. On the other hand, for products that contain ingredients with addictive properties such as codeine, the prices of these products on the streets are up to 1000 times more than their normal prices in pharmacies [110–114].

Due to patents and intellectual properties' infringements, there are economic risks quantifiable in loss incurred by legitimate retail businesses licensed to trade in medicines. Several legitimate companies are deprived of their rightful profits due to the unjust competition from unlicensed businesses and non-professionals [115, 116].

The financial loss resulting from counterfeiting of medicines is huge and appears to be increasing annually. Estimates from WHO are that about 32 billion US dollars were lost to drug counterfeiting business in 2004; increasing to 40 billion US dollars in 2006 and it was expected to reach 75 billion US dollars by 2010 [110, 117].

It should be remembered that every dollar spent on buying a medicine from an unlicensed entity, it is a dollar lost by a legitimate business that is paying taxes to the government. Most importantly, every dollar spent on a substandard medicine is money lost by the consumer that should have been used to buy a genuine medicine that has some guaranteed potential of healing rather than the high probability of harm from counterfeit product or a product not stored in appropriate conditions.

6.3. Promotion of abuse and misuse of medicines

Unlicensed traders of medicines and non-professionals promote the abuse and misuse of medicines by increasing the availability, accessibility and sometimes affordability of prescription and non-prescription drugs. By making it easier for people to get the medicines without any control, these traders facilitate to feed the habits of people affected by the abuse condition [118–121].

It is should be noted that drug or medicine misuse refers to the use of a drug for purposes for which it was not intended or using a drug in excessive quantities; drug abuse is the misuse of prescription or over-the-counter drugs with negative consequences such as addiction, decreased performance at work, and or with problems at work, school, home or in interpersonal relationships or problems with the law. People misuse or abuse OTCs and prescription drugs as a result of being previously given them for a specific ailment or by being influenced by friends or family members [120–123].

The cycle of abuse may start because getting a prescription means paying a private practitioner or a prescriber or spending time in long queues at public health facilities; people make a shortcut by buying from the streets. Because people continue to buy, informal traders or unlicensed entities feel vindicated to acquire more stock for their clients. This situation in turn encourage the middle suppliers and ultimately the manufacturers or criminals to get the stock or manufacture these substandard or counterfeit medicines in order to meet the needs for their niche markets [124].

The most common medicines abused are codeine-based (especially compounded analgesics) medicines, cough products (particularly containing dextromethorphan), sedative antihistamines, decongestants and laxatives as well as medicines used to increase or decrease appetite; to enhance sexual performance such as Viagra® and antibiotics. Of great concern is the abuse of opioids or narcotic drugs that are controlled drugs normally obtainable only with a prescription. Given the addictive properties of these medicines, patients sometimes pressurise their healthcare providers to prescribe these products to them, hence triggering the cycle of abuse [125–127].

6.4. Antibiotic resistance and treatment failure

One of the most damaging consequences of informal trading of medicines is the widespread facilitation of the misuse of antibiotics as unlicensed traders make them available to the general public. The unrestricted use of antibiotics combined with the diminished quality or potency of products sold due to improper storage conditions create an environment ripe for the onset of antibiotic resistance. Furthermore, counterfeit antibiotics with low amount of actual active antibiotics or worse with no active ingredient at all are even more dangerous for three reasons, and they provide false assurance and hope to the sick people who believe that they are being treated; they thus delay the actual treatment and thus provide the germs the time to multiply and aggravate the condition; and finally, if in low doses they provide the germs with the means to develop resistance. It is documented that resistance to malaria medicines, anti-tuberculosis, antiretroviral drugs and other infections has resulted from such instances [116, 128, 129].

It goes without saying that the ultimate outcome will be treatment failure. Some experts believe that germs' resistance stemming from substandard, falsified and counterfeit drugs has contributed a lot to the current stalemate in the fight against malaria and tuberculosis in developing countries. Furthermore, when treatment failure is experienced by patients after using medicines they got from public health facilities, it leads them to lose confidence in the healthcare system and sadly this forces them to resort to alternative sources of drugs including informal market or alternative treatment modalities including traditional medicine which is also ill-equipped to deal with deadly diseases such as malaria, HIV and tuberculosis. Hence, it is not surprising that an estimated 700,000 deaths per year are believed to be caused by fake antimalarial and anti-tuberculosis products [130–136].

6.5. Adverse drug reactions

Adverse drug reactions (ADRs) leading to hospitalisations have been reported as a result of the consumption of medicines obtained from non-licensed businesses and non-professionals. Although the advent of ADRs is a normal occurrence even when using legitimate drugs, informally obtained drugs carry added risks due to improper storage, uncertain quality, and incorrect use as a result of the lack of professional oversight [137–139].

6.6. Fatalities

Several fatal cases have been documented resulting from the consumption of medicines of dubious quality brought from unlicensed entities. Reports of acute poisoning resulting from counterfeit, adultered, substandard or falsified drugs abound. Hundreds of deaths from acute renal failure due to poisoning from diethylene glycol in cough syrups have been reported in Haiti, Bangladesh, Nigeria, India and Argentina. The following cases illustrate the range and scale of circumstances in various countries. In Pakistan, 107 people died as a result of consuming a contaminated product made of isosorbide and very high amounts of pyrimethamine. In Niger, about 2500 people had died following the administration of counterfeit meningococcal-vaccines (containing no active ingredient) that was administered to some 60,000 people during the 1995 meningitis epidemic. In China, by the end of 2001, about 192,000 people were reported to have died as a result of the utilisation of fake medicinal products. Furthermore, in 2007/2008, a tainted Chinese crude heparin product killed 149 persons in 11 different countries including 81 deaths in the USA [140–158]. The above suggest that several other deaths due to products traded informally by unlicensed entities and non-professionals go unnoticed, unreported and unaccounted for.

7. Suggested strategies to mitigate risks associated with illegal and informal trade of medicines

The scale of the consequences from illegal and informal trading of medicines by unlicensed businesses and non-professionals ought to galvanise a resolve and a strong response from the international community of nations. Several international resolutions and initiatives have been implemented as far back as over two decades ago with a focus on counterfeiting. Given the trajectory that the business of counterfeiting and its associated spin-offs such as terrorism, it is time to rethink the concessions that were made by parliamentarians of several nations to take out the control of the trade of medicines from pharmacists or more specifically from their national pharmaceutical regulatory controls [159–163].

Everyone agrees that medicines are not ordinary commodities; the fact is that most of them are potent at doses expressed in milligrams, that is, in very small quantities; their abuse brings too much suffering and problems to society. On the contrary, when appropriately managed, controlled, prescribed, dispensed and used correctly, they relieve mankind of many of its diseases, suffering and thus contribute to happiness, the ultimate search for every soul on the planet earth.

Although several strategies may be and will be suggested to address the risks and consequences of illegal international and national trading of medicines, none requires more courage from decision-makers than taking the stand and saying that 'enough is enough'. The trade of medicines should be professionalised and regulated in such a way that the illegal trade will scare most amateurs trying to get into it; that street-vending of medicines will not only be outlawed but completely eliminated as it is made to be unproductive and unsustainable [164, 165].

The courage needed to address the consequences of illegal trading of medicines should be great as the courage that the world summoned to establish the United Nations, the Global

http://dx.doi.org/10.5772/66471

Fund and other institutions that have made a difference to the world. What is really said here is that the fight against illegal trading of medicines as well as the production and sale of drugs of abuse should be a top priority for ministries of health, finances and justice of nations of the world [140, 166]. The belief that current and existing national and international interventions suffice to handle this problem is clearly contradicted by the facts on the grounds.

The situation demands that some innovative ways should be found and a rethink of the interventions already implemented. Some suggestions are given below.

7.1. Going back to basics—restoring the mandate of trade of medicines to professionals

There should be a concerted effort from international trading blocks and institutions to support their constituencies to revise, review, amend or update their legislations and/or regulations in order incorporate with no ambiguity the stand that 'no one will trade in medicines unless he is properly licensed with a verifiable physical address and meet criteria defined in existing good practices governing the procurement and sale of medicines in international trade'. This should also include specific regulations on maintenance of traceability of all categories of finished medicinal and health products as well as of excipients and other raw materials used in the production of medicines.

7.2. Revamping national and international legislations—outlaw double standards

The double standard entrenched in several national legislations that essentially allow national manufacturers to export their substandard products to other countries should be repelled. Moreover, parallel trade, which is one of the causes of foiling of traceability of products as a result of manipulations legally permissible, should be revised with clear instructions and legally binding standards to ensure that the traceability of the products and their sources is maintained.

7.3. Implement severe punishments and penalties

Concurrently, punishments and penalties for infringements should exclude options for paying fines but increase the harshness of penalties as deterrent. Furthermore, international cooperation and collaborative investigations on existing criminal syndicates, sharing of related information between law-enforcing agencies should be enhanced.

7.4. Encourage local production and strengthen national QA systems

Put in place mechanisms to encourage priority local production of products that lend themselves to local production because of the existence of raw materials and skills base; and mechanisms that foster quality assurance systems strengthening in countries with weaker systems. Foster a good neighbourhood culture that discourages undue and unfair competition but supports collaborative efforts that ensure accessibility and availability of good quality medicines. Most importantly, all countries should establish market surveillance through their scientific institutions, academia and/with the assistance of legitimate manufacturers who are willing to be involved in the fight.

7.5. Online pharmacies to be restricted to defined territories and prohibited to trade internationally

As extreme as it sounds, the experience of the past decades have shown that oversight of online pharmacies' operations has proved difficult. Although, the suggested restrictions might not be implemented by concerned pharmacies, the key here is that the enforcements of heavy penalties when deviations have been uncovered is what is sought here.

7.6. Robust, unrelenting and consistent public health education campaigns

There is a need to develop educational materials with clear messages targeting public health officials and health care practitioners, customs' officials, the youth and consumers at large, on the dangers of inappropriately stored, substandard, falsified or counterfeit products; as well as on how to identify quality marks on genuine products. The campaigns should be launched in various media including national theatrical performances, radios, television and newsprints.

7.7. International blacklisting of rogue, unscrupulous and non-conforming manufacturers, wholesalers and distributors of medicines

It is suggested here that, just as there is an international database of clinical trials, an international database of companies, businesses and entities that have been confirmed as aiding, assisting, contributing to the trade of substandard, falsified and counterfeit drugs or practicing outside the regulatory limits of good practices, should be instituted as a way of shaming these enterprises and alerting buyers not to buy from or trade with them.

8. Concluding remarks

This review has highlighted the origins, the rationale and the risks associated with the trading of medicines by unlicensed organisations and non-professionals. These risks include the criminal poisoning, the production and sale of counterfeit medicines, unfair competition, encouraging abuse and misuse of medicines, and treatment failure as well as fatalities. The major findings are that concessions made to allow non-licensed businesses and non-professionals to trade in medicines have resulted in several consequences that are threatening the whole world. It is this realisation that has prompted the recommendation that courage from decision-makers is required for them to take a stand and hand over back the trading of medicines firmly in the hands of licensed professionals while outlawing loopholes that sustained the trade of medicines by unlicensed entities and non-professionals.

Author details

Ntambwe Malangu

Address all correspondence to: gustavmalangu@gmail.com

School of Public Health, Sefako Makgatho Health Sciences University, Pretoria, South Africa

References

[1] Nunn JF. (2002). Egyptian Medicine. University of Okhlahoma Press, USA.

[2] Harding G and Taylor KMG. (2015). Pharmacy Practice. 2nd Edition, CRC Press, New York, USA.

[3] Anderson S. (2001). The historical context of pharmacy. In: Taylor K, Harding G, editors. Pharmacy practice. London: Taylor & Francis.ISBN 0203303156.

[4] Malangu N. 1400 to 1900: Diseases, Endemic. Cultural Sociology of the Middle East, Asia, and Africa: An Encyclopedia [9781412981767]: Volume 2: Africa. Edited by Edward Ramsamy. Sage Publications Inc.

[5] Curth, L. H. [Ed.]. (2006). From Physick to Pharmacology: Five Hundred Years of Drug Retailing. Ashgate Publishing, Ltd.

[6] Anderson S. (2005).Making medicines: a brief history of pharmacy and pharmaceuticals. London: Pharmaceutical Press. ISBN 0853695970.

[7] Walvin, J. (2013). Crossings: Africa, the Americas and the Atlantic Slave Trade. Reaktion Books, USA

[8] Anderson S. The state of the world's pharmacy: a portrait of the pharmacy profession. J Interprof Care. 2002;16(4):391–404.

[9] Malangu N. Prehistory to 1400: Diseases, Endemic. Cultural Sociology of the Middle East, and Africa: An Encyclopedia [9781412981767]: Volume 2: Africa. Edited by Edward Ramsamy. Sage Publications Inc.

[10] Settles Joshua Dwayne. (1996). The Impact of Colonialism on African Economic Development". University of Tennessee Honors Thesis Projects. Available at: http://trace.tennessee.edu/utk_chanhonoproj/182.

[11] McAllister, W. B. (2000). Drug Diplomacy in the Twentieth Century: An International History. Psychology Press

[12] Miers, S., & Kopytoff, I. (1979). Slavery in Africa: historical and anthropological perspectives. University of Wisconsin Press, USA.

[13] Braudel, F. (1995). A History of Civilizations (pp. 309–310). Penguin Books, New York.

[14] Last, M., & Chavunduka, G. L. (1986). The Professionalisation of African Medicine (No. 1). Manchester University Press.

[15] Lewis, M., & MacLeod, R. (1988). Medical politics and the professionalisation of medicine in New South Wales, 1850–1901. *Journal of Australian Studies, 12(22), 69–82.*

[16] Du Bois, W. E. B. (1965). The World and Africa: An Inquiry into the Part Which Africa Has Played in World History. International Publishers Company.

[17] Corfield, P. J. (2009). From poison peddlers to civic worthies: The reputation of the apothecaries in Georgian England. Social History of Medicine.

[18] Deacon, H. (2004). Medical gentlemen and the process of professionalisation before 1860. *Clio Medica/The Wellcome Series in the History of Medicine, 74(1), 85–103.*

[19] Roberts, M. J. (2009). The politics of professionalization: MPs, medical men, and the 1858 Medical Act. *Medical History, 53(01), 37–56.*

[20] Kam, T. W. (2011). Professionalization of Chinese Medicine Development in Hong Kong: The Post-handover Experiences. *International Journal of Health, Wellness & Society, 1(3):50–52*

[21] Digby, A. (2002). Making a medical living: doctors and patients in the English market for medicine, 1720–1911. Cambridge University Press.

[22] Qiu, J. (2007)). Traditional medicine: a culture in the balance. *Nature, 448(7150), 126–128.*

[23] Porter, R. (1995). Disease, medicine and society in England, 1550-1860. Cambridge University Press.

[24] Abdullahi, A. A. (2011). Trends and challenges of traditional medicine in Africa. *African Journal of Traditional, Complementary and Alternative Medicines, 8(5S).*

[25] Digby, A. (2005). Self-medication and the trade in medicine within a multi-ethnic context: a case study of South Africa from the mid-nineteenth to mid-twentieth centuries. *Social History of Medicine, 18(3), 439–457.*

[26] de Roubaix, M. (2016). The decolonialisation of medicine in South Africa: Threat or opportunity? *SAMJ: South African Medical Journal, 106(2), 159–161.*

[27] Lowe, R. F., & Montagu, D. (2009). Legislation, regulation, and consolidation in the retail pharmacy sector in low-income countries. *Southern Med Review, 2(2), 35–44.*

[28] Anderson, S. (2002). The state of the world's pharmacy: a portrait of the pharmacy profession. *Journal of Interprofessional Care, 16(4), 391–404.*

[29] Barber, N. (1993). Drugs: from prescription only to pharmacy only. *BMJ: British Medical Journal, 307(6905), 640.*

[30] Malangu, N., & Ogunbanjo, G. A. (2006). Predictors of topical steroid misuse among patrons of pharmacies in Pretoria. *South African Family Practice, 48(1), 14–14e.*

[31] Kildemoes, H. W., Sørensen, H. T., & Hallas, J. (2011). The Danish national prescription registry. *Scandinavian Journal of Publish Health, 39(7 suppl), 38–41.*

[32] Greenwood, J., & Ronit, K. (1991). Pharmaceutical regulation in Denmark and the UK: Reformulating interest representation to the transnational level. *European Journal of Political Research, 19(2–3), 327–359.*

[33] Myers, B., Siegfried, N., & Parry, C. D. (2003). Over-the-counter and prescription medicine misuse in Cape Town-findings from specialist treatment centres. *South African Medical Journal, 93(5), 367–370.*

[34] WHO. Assessment of medicines regulatory systems in Sub-Saharan African countries: an overview of findings from 26 assessment reports. WHO, Geneva, 2010

[35] Worthen, D. B. (2005). Pharmaceutical Legislation: An Historical Perspective. *International Journal of Pharmaceutical Compounding, 10(1), 20–28.*

[36] Mrazek, M., & Mossialos, E. (2004). Regulating pharmaceutical prices in the European Union. Regulating pharmaceuticals in Europe: striving for efficiency, equity and quality. European Observatory on Health Systems and Policies, Copenhagen. 114–129.

[37] Rago L. and Santoso B. (2003). Drug Regulation: History, Present and Future. Available at: http://www.who.int/medicines/technical_briefing/tbs/Drug_Regulation

[38] Videau JV. (2001). Editorial: Making Medicines Safe. Bulletin of the World Health Organization, 79(2).

[39] Okie, S. (2009). Multinational medicines—ensuring drug quality in an era of global manufacturing. *New England Journal of Medicine, 361(8), 737-740.*

[40] Patterson, D. A. (2009). Local Borders and Global Flows: Senegal's Illegal Pharmaceutical Trade. *Africa Policy Journal, 6, 21.*

[41] Kuehn BM. (2011). As production goes global, drug supply faces greater risks to safety, quality. *JAMA, 306(8), 811–813.*

[42] Ames, J., & Souza, D. Z. (2012). Counterfeiting of drugs in Brazil. *Revista de Saúde Pública, 46(1), 154–159.*

[43] Ravinetto R and Schiavetti B. (2015) The quality of medicines: an ethical issue? *Indian J Med Ethics, 12(4), 232–234.*

[44] Bate R et al. (2010) Medicine registration and medicine quality: a preliminary analysis of key cities in emerging markets. *Research and Reports in Tropical Medicine, 1, 89–93.*

[45] Glynn, D. (2009). The effects of parallel trade on affordable access to medicines. *Eurohealth, 15(2), 1–4.*

[46] Gostin, L. O., Buckley, G. J., & Kelley, P. W. (2013). Stemming the global trade in falsified and substandard medicines. *JAMA, 309(16), 1693–1694.*

[47] Dyer, O. (2014). Drugs exported from India to Africa are poorer quality than those sent elsewhere. *BMJ, 349, g6017.*

[48] Kuehn, B. M. (2013). IOM: Curbing fake drugs will require national tracking and global teamwork. *JAMA, 3, 309(13), 1333–4.*

[49] Ubajaka, C. F., Obi-Okaro, A. C., Emelumadu, O. F., Azumarah, M. N., Ukegbu, A. U., & Ilikannu, S. O. (2016). Factors Associated with Drug Counterfeit in Nigeria: A Twelve Year Review. *British Journal of Medicine & Medical Research, 12(4), 1–8.*

[50] Chika, A., Bello S. O, Jimoh A. O., and Umar, M. T. (2011). The Menace of fake drugs: Consequences, causes and possible solutions. *Research Journal of Medical Sciences, 5 (5): 257–261.*

[51] Baxerres, C., & Le Hesran, J. Y. (2011). Where do pharmaceuticals on the market originate? An analysis of the informal drug supply in Cotonou, Benin. *Social Science & Medicine, 73(8), 1249–1256.*

[52] Vitell SJ., Rawwas, M. Y., & Festervand, T. A. (1991). The business ethics of pharmacists: conflicts practices and beliefs. *Journal of Business Ethics, 10(4), 295–301.*

[53] Ziemer T. (2015). Falsified medicines in Africa. *The Lancet Global Health, 3, e82.*

[54] Binagwaho A, Bate R, Gasana M, Karema C, Mucyo Y, et al. (2013). Combatting Substandard and Falsified Medicines: A View from Rwanda. *PLoS Medicine, 10(7), e1001476.*

[55] Rago L. et al. (2014). Review. Regulatory framework for access to safe, effective, quality medicines. *Antiviral Therapy, 19(Suppl 3), 69–77.*

[56] Raustiala, K., & Slaughter, A. M. (2002). International law, international relations and compliance. International Relations and Compliance. *Princeton Law & Public Affairs Paper, 2:2.*

[57] Staiger, R. W., & Sykes, A. O. (2011). International trade, national treatment, and domestic regulation. *The Journal of Legal Studies, 40(1), 149–203.*

[58] Dhalla IA et A.S. (2008). Detsky, risks and benefits of importing prescription medications from lower-income countries. *JAMA, 300(12), 1453–1455.*

[59] Gøtzsche, P. C., Smith, R., & Rennie, D. (2013). Deadly medicines and organised crime: how Big Pharma has corrupted healthcare. Radcliffe, London, UK.

[60] Reynolds, L., & McKee, M. (2010). Organised crime and the efforts to combat it: a concern for public health. *Globalization and health, 6(1), 1.*

[61] Rago L. et al. (2014). Review. Regulatory framework for access to safe, effective, quality medicines. *Antiviral Therapy, 19(Suppl 3), 69–77.*

[62] Liang, B. A. (2006). Fade to black: importation and counterfeit drugs. *American Journal of Law & Medicine, 32, 279.*

[63] Davison, M. (2011). Pharmaceutical anti-counterfeiting: combating the real danger from fake drugs. John Wiley & Sons.

[64] Goyal, A., 2015. 'Pharmacy of the World'is ill?. *Developing world bioethics*, 15(1), pp.ii-ii.

[65] Newton, P. N., Tabernero, P., Dwivedi, P., Culzoni, M. J., Monge, M. E., Swamidoss, I., … & Simao, J. (2014). Falsified medicines in Africa: all talk, no action.

[66] Newton, P. N., Green, M. D., Mildenhall, D. C., Plançon, A., Nettey, H., Nyadong, et al. (2011). Poor quality vital anti-malarials in Africa-an urgent neglected public health priority. *Malaria Journal, 10(1), 1.*

[67] Mali DK, Mitkare SS, Moon RS, & Kshirsagar R. (2011). Anti-counterfeit packaging in pharma industry: review. *International Journal Pharmacy Pharmaceutical Science, 3, 46.*

[68] Nayyar, G. M., Breman, J. G., Newton, P. N., & Herrington, J. (2012). Poor-quality antimalarial drugs in South-East Asia and sub-Saharan Africa. *The Lancet Infectious Diseases, 12(6), 488–496.*

[69] Wise J. (2013). Record number of fake drugs are seized in crackdown. *BMJ, 346, f4204.*

[70] Widdowson, D. [2013). Bordering on corruption: an analysis of corrupt customs practices that impact the trading community. *World Customs Journal, 7(2).*

[71] Shakoor O et al. (1997). Assessment of the incidence of substandard drugs in developing countries. *Tropical Medicine and International Health,* 2(9), *839–845.*

[72] Ponsaers, P., Shapland, J., & Williams, C. C. (2008). Does the informal economy link to organised crime? *International Journal of Social Economics, 35*(9), *644–650.*

[73] Mackey, T. K., & Liang, B. A. (2013). Global reach of direct-to-consumer advertising using social media for illicit online drug sales. *Journal of medical Internet research, 15(5), e105.*

[74] Liang, B. A., & Mackey, T. K. (2013). Online availability and safety of drugs in shortage: a descriptive study of internet vendor characteristics. *Survey of Anesthesiology, 57(1), 54–55.*

[75] Dégardin, K., Roggo, Y., & Margot, P. (2014). Understanding and fighting the medicine counterfeit market. *Journal of Pharmaceutical and Biomedical Analysis, 87, 167–175.*

[76] Oji, V., Weaver, S. B., Falade, D., & Fagbemi, B. (2014). Emerging Roles of US Pharmacists in Global Health and Africa. *Journal of Biosafety & Health Education.*

[77] Wafula, F., Abuya, T., Amin, A., & Goodman, C. (2014). The policy-practice gap: describing discordances between regulation on paper and real-life practices among specialized drug shops in Kenya. *BMC Health Services Research, 14(1), 1.*

[78] Cohn, J., Von Schoenen-Angerer, T., Jambert, E., Arreghini, G and Childs, M. (2012). When falsified medicines enter the supply chain: Description of an incident in Kenya and lessons learned for rapid response. *Journal of Public Health Policy, 1–9.*

[79] Bate R., Hess K. (2012). The role of pre-shipment batch testing in ensuring good medicine quality. *MWJ, 3:12.*

[80] Erhun, W. O., Babalola, O. O., & Erhun, M. O. (2001). Drug regulation and control in Nigeria: The challenge of counterfeit drugs. *Journal of Health & Population in Developing Countries, 4(2), 23–34.*

[81] Deisingh, A. K. (2005). Pharmaceutical counterfeiting. *Analyst, 130(3), 271–279.*

[82] McGregor A. (1997). Counterfeit's drugs flood developing world. *The Lancet, 350(9092), 1690.*

[83] Mackey, T. K., & Liang, B. A. (2011). The global counterfeit drug trade: patient safety and public health risks. *Journal of Pharmaceutical Sciences, 100(11), 4571–4579.*

[84] Kaur, H., Goodman, C., Thompson, E., Thompson, K. A., Masanja, I., et al. (2008). A Nationwide Survey of the Quality of Antimalarials in Retail Outlets in Tanzania. *PLoS One, 3(10), e3403.*

[85] Worley, J., & Hall, J. M. (2012). Doctor shopping: a concept analysis. *Research and Theory for Nursing Practice, 26(4), 262–278.*

[86] Bucci, R. V. (2014). Medical Business Law and Regulations. In Medicine and Business (pp. 161-–170). Springer International Publishing.

[87] Rigg, K. K., Kurtz, S. P., & Surratt, H. L. (2012). Patterns of prescription medication diversion among drug dealers. *Drugs: Education, Prevention and Policy, 19(2), 145–155.*

[88] Green, T. C., Bowman, S. E., Ray, M., Zaller, N., Heimer, R., & Case, P. (2013). Collaboration or coercion? Partnering to divert prescription opioid medications. *Journal of Urban Health, 90(4), 758–767.*

[89] Berge, K. H., Dillon, K. R., Sikkink, K. M., Taylor, T. K., & Lanier, W. L. (2012). Diversion of drugs within health care facilities, a multiple-victim crime: patterns of diversion, scope, consequences, detection, and prevention. *In Mayo Clinic Proceedings, 87(7), 674–682.*

[90] Nargiso, J. E., Ballard, E. L., & Skeer, M. R. (2015). A systematic review of risk and protective factors associated with nonmedical use of prescription drugs among youth in the United States: a social ecological perspective. *Journal of Studies on Alcohol and Drugs, 76(1), 5–20.*

[91] Malangu N. Risk factors and outcomes of food poisoning in Africa. In" Significance, Prevention and Control of Food Related Diseases. Edited by Hussaini Anthony Makun. doi:10.5772/60612

[92] Poorolajal, J., Haghtalab, T., Farhadi, M., & Darvishi, N. (2015). Substance use disorder and risk of suicidal ideation, suicide attempt and suicide death: a meta-analysis. *Journal of Public Health, fdv148.*

[93] Jackson, G., Patel, S., & Khan, S. (2012). Assessing the problem of counterfeit medications in the United Kingdom. *International Journal of Clinical Practice, 66(3), 241–250.*

[94] Lee, H., Hsu, C. C., Chen, F. L., Yen, Y. Y., Lin, P. L., Chiu, Y. W., Huang, H. L. et al. (2014). Area disparity in children's perceptions of access to tobacco and cigarette purchasing experiences in Taiwan. *Journal of School Health, 84(8), 507–515.*

[95] Holstein, B. E., Hansen, E. H., Due, P., & Almarsdóttir, A. B. (2003). Self-reported medicine use among 11-to 15-year-old girls and boys in Denmark 1988-1998. *Scandinavian Journal of Public Health, 31(5), 334–341.*

[96] Amoako, R. (2014). Illicit drug use among Finnish children: channels of acquisition (Thesis).

[97] Oshikoya KA and Senbajo I.O.(2010). Medicines turned poison for children in Nigeria. *West African Journal of Medicine, 29(4), 278–279.*

[98] Clift, C. (2010). Combating counterfeit, falsified and substandard medicines: defining the way forward? Chatham House, London, UK.

[99] WHO-Impact. Declaration of Roma, 18th February2006. Conclusions and recommendations of the WHO "Combating Counterfeit Drugs: Building Effective International Collaboration". *International Conference - Rome, Italy 16–18 February 2006.*

[100] Duthel, H. (2015). Illegal drug trade-The War on Drugs: Drug trade generated an estimated US $531.6 billion in 2013. BoD–Books on Demand.

[101] Orizio, G., Schulz, P., Domenighini, S., Caimi, L., Rosati, C., Rubinelli, S., & Gelatti, U. (2009). Cyberdrugs: a cross-sectional study of online pharmacies characteristics. *The European Journal of Public Health, 19(4), 375–377.*

[102] Stecher, V. J., Jackson, G., Banks, I., Arver, S., & Greenall, W. (2010). Analysis of Pharmaceuticals Seized by Authorities in the United Kingdom for Suspicion of Being Counterfeit VIAGRA®. *ISMH World Congress 2010 Abstract 125.*

[103] Siva N. (2010). Tackling the booming trade in counterfeit drugs. *Lancet, 376, 1725–1726.*

[104] Tomic S. et al. (2010). Identification of counterfeit medicines for erectile dysfunction from an illegal supply chain. *Arh Hig Rada Toksikol, 61, 69–75.*

[105] Sidley, P. (2008). South Africa withdraws TB drugs because of quality concerns. *British Medical Journal, 337, a1385.*

[106] Akunyili, D. N. (2012). The War Against Counterfeit Medicine. African Books Collective.

[107] Jack, A. (2007). Counterfeit medicines. Bitter pills. *BMJ, 335, 1120–1121.*

[108] Swaminath G. (2008). Faking it—The menace of counterfeit Drugs. *Indian Journal of Psychiatry, 50(4), 238–240.*

[109] Bate, R., Jin, G. Z., Mathur, A., & Attaran, A. (2016). Poor-Quality Drugs and Global Trade: A Pilot Study. *American Journal of Health Economics.*

[110] Blackstone, E. A., Fuhr Jr, J. P., & Pociask, S. (2014). The health and economic effects of counterfeit drugs. *American Health & Drug Benefits, 7(4).*

[111] Bate R., Jin, G. Z., & Mathur, A. (2015). Falsified or substandard? Assessing price and non-price signals of drug quality. *Journal of Economics & Management Strategy, 24(4), 687–711.*

[112] Burki T. (2010). The real cost of counterfeit medicines. *The Lancet Infectious Diseases, 10, 585–586.*

[113] Moken, M. C. (2003). Fake pharmaceuticals: How they and relevant legislation or lack thereof contribute to consistently high and increasing drug prices. *American Journal of Medicine, 29, 525.*

[114] Mendis, S., Fukino, K., Cameron, A., Laing, R., Filipe Jr, A., Khatib, O., ... & Ewen, M. (2007). The availability and affordability of selected essential medicines for chronic diseases in six low-and middle-income countries. *Bulletin of the World Health Organization, 85(4), 279–288.*

[115] Gostin, L. O., & Buckley, G. J. (Eds.). (2013). Countering the problem of falsified and substandard drugs. National Academies Press.

[116] Fink, C., Maskus, K. E., & Qian, Y. (2016). The economic effects of counterfeiting and piracy: a review and implications for developing countries. *The World Bank Research Observer, 31(1), 1–28.*

[117] WHO, 2006. Counterfeit medicines. Fact Sheet Revised. November 14, 2006. Available at: http://www.who.int/medicines/services.

[118] Frauger, E., Nordmann, S., Orleans, V., Pradel, V., Pauly, V., Thirion, X., & Micallef, J. (2012). Which psychoactive prescription drugs are illegally obtained and through which ways of acquisition? About OPPIDUM survey. *Fundamental & Clinical Pharmacology, 26(4), 549–556.*

[119] Johanson, C. E., Arfken, C. L., di Menza, S., & Schuster, C. R. (2012). Diversion and abuse of buprenorphine: findings from national surveys of treatment patients and physicians. *Drug and Alcohol Dependence, 120(1), 190–195.*

[120] Casati, A., Sedefov, R., & Pfeiffer-Gerschel, T. (2012). Misuse of medicines in the European Union: a systematic review of the literature. *European Addiction Research, 18(5), 228–245.*

[121] Malangu, N., & Ogunbanjo, G. A. (2006). Predictors of topical steroid misuse among patrons of pharmacies in Pretoria. *South African Family Practice, 48(1), 14–14e.*

[122] Odejide, A. O. (2006). Status of drug use/abuse in Africa: A review. *International Journal of Mental Health and Addiction, 4(2), 87–102.*

[123] Malangu, N. (2007). Self-reported use of traditional, complementary and over-the-counter medicines by HIV-infected patients on antiretroviral therapy in Pretoria, South Africa. *African Journal of Traditional, Complementary and Alternative Medicines, 4(3), 273–278.*

[124] Garland, E. L., Froeliger, B., Zeidan, F., Partin, K., & Howard, M. O. (2013). The downward spiral of chronic pain, prescription opioid misuse, and addiction: Cognitive, affective, and neuropsychopharmacologic pathways. *Neuroscience & Biobehavioral Reviews, 37(10), 2597–2607.*

[125] Nelson, M. E., Bryant, S. M., & Aks, S. E. (2014). Emerging drugs of abuse. *Emergency Medicine Clinics of North America, 32(1), 1–28.*

[126] Abbott, F. V., & Fraser, M. I. (1998). Use and abuse of over-the-counter analgesic agents. *Journal of Psychiatry and Neuroscience, 23(1), 13.*

[127] Bardo, M. T., Neisewander, J. L., & Kelly, T. H. (2013). Individual differences and social influences on the neurobehavioral pharmacology of abused drugs. *Pharmacological Reviews, 65(1), 255–290.*

[128] Shindo, Y., Ito, R., Kobayashi, D., Ando, M., Ichikawa, M., Shiraki, A., Yamaguchi, I. et al. (2013). Risk factors for drug-resistant pathogens in community-acquired and healthcare-associated pneumonia. *American Journal of Respiratory and Critical Care Medicine, 188(8), 985–995.*

[129] Laxminarayan, R., Duse, A., Wattal, C., Zaidi, A. K., Wertheim, H. F., Sumpradit, N., Greko, C., et al. (2013). Antibiotic resistance—the need for global solutions. *The Lancet Infectious Diseases, 13(12), 1057–1098*

[130] Skrahina, A., Hurevich, H., Zalutskaya, A., Sahalchyk, E., Astrauko, A., Hoffner, S., van Gemert, W., et al. (2013). Multidrug-resistant tuberculosis in Belarus: the size of the problem and associated risk factors. *Bulletin of the World Health Organization, 91(1), 36–45.*

[131] Roca, I., Akova, M., Baquero, F., Carlet, J., Cavaleri, M., Coenen, S., ... & Kahlmeter, G. (2015). The global threat of antimicrobial resistance: science for intervention. *New Microbes and New Infections, 6, 22–29.*

[132] Woolhouse, M., Ward, M., van Bunnik, B., & Farrar, J. (2015). Antimicrobial resistance in humans, livestock and the wider environment. *Philosophical Transactions of the Royal Society B, 370(1670), 201400–201483.*

[133] Holmes, A. H., Moore, L. S. P., Sundsfjord, A., et al. (2016). Understanding the mechanisms and drivers of antimicrobial resistance. *Lancet, 387, 176–187.*

[134] Amon, J. J. (2008). Dangerous medicine. Unproven AIDS cures and counterfeit antiretroviral drugs. *Globalization and Health, 4, 5.*

[135] Kimang'a, A. N. (2012). A situational analysis of antimicrobial drug resistance in Africa: are we losing the battle? *Ethiopian Journal of Health Sciences, 22(2).*

[136] Adelani, T. W., Oluyedun, H. A., & Ayinla, I. M. A. (2015). Assessment of the government's mea antibiotics and antima. I***nternational Journal of Current Science and Technology 3(7):37-40.***

[137] Angamo, M. T., Chalmers, L., Curtain, C. M., & Bereznicki, L. R. (2016). Adverse-drug-reaction-related hospitalisations in developed and developing countries: A review of prevalence and contributing factors. *Drug Safety, 39(9), 847–857.*

[138] Alomar, M. J. (2014). Factors affecting the development of adverse drug reactions. *Saudi Pharmaceutical Journal: SPJ: the official publication of the Saudi Pharmaceutical Society, 22, 83–94.*

[139] Tremblay, M. (2013). Medicines counterfeiting is a complex problem: a review of key challenges across the supply chain. *Current Drug Safety, 8(1), 43–55.*

[140] Wertheimer, A. I., & Norris, J. (2009). Safeguarding against substandard-counterfeit drugs: mitigating a macroeconomic pandemic. *Research in Social and Administrative Pharmacy, 5(1), 4–16.*

[141] Nsimba, S. E. (2009). Problems associated with substandard and counterfeit drugs in developing countries: A review article on global implications of counterfeit drugs in the era of anti-retroviral (ARVS) drugs in a free market economy.

[142] Akunyili, D. N., & Nnani, I. P. (2004). Risk of medicines: Counterfeit drugs. *International Journal of Risk & Safety in Medicine, 16(3), 181–190.*

[143] Kelesidis, T., Kelesidis, I., Rafailidis, P. I., & Falagas, M. E. (2007). Counterfeit or substandard antimicrobial drugs: a review of the scientific evidence. *Journal of Antimicrobial Chemotherapy, 60(2), 214–236.*

[144] Jha, A. K., Prasopa-Plaizier, N., Larizgoitia, I., & Bates, D. W. (2010). Patient safety research: an overview of the global evidence. *Quality and Safety in Health Care, 19(1), 42–47.*

[145] Cockburn, R., Newton, P. N., Agyarko, E. K., Akunyili, D., & White, N. J. (2005). The global threat of counterfeit drugs: why industry and governments must communicate the dangers. *PLoS Med, 2(4), e100.*

[146] Aldhous, P. (2005). Counterfeit pharmaceuticals: murder by medicine. *Nature, 434(7030), 132–136.*

[147] Newton, P. N., Green, M. D., Fernández, F. M., Day, N. P., & White, N. J. (2006). Counterfeit anti-infective drugs. *The Lancet Infectious Diseases, 6(9), 602–613.*

[148] Morris, J., & Stevens, P. (2006). Counterfeit Medicines in Less Developed Countries. International Policy Network, London, May 3, 6.

[149] Lewis, K. (2009). China's counterfeit medicine trade booming. *Canadian Medical Association Journal, 181(10), E237–E238.*

[150] Scalzo, AJ. (1996). The 1996 Haitian epidemic. *Journal of Toxicology and Clinical Toxicology, 34(5), 513–516.*

[151] Senior, K. (2008). Global health-care implications of substandard medicines. *The Lancet, 8, 666.*

[152] Singh, J. et al. (2001). Diethylene glycol poisoning in Gurgaon, India. *Bulletin of the World Health Organization, 79(2), 88–95.*

[153] Dorlo T. (2015). Falsified and substandard antimalarials. A fatal threat to malaria control. *Mtb. Bull Nederlands Soc Trop Med Int Health, 53(3), 13–19.*

[154] Harugeri, A., Parthasarathi, G., Ramesh, M., Sharma, J., & Devi, D. P. (2008). Story of heparin recall: What India can do? *Journal of Postgraduate Medicine, 54(3), 222.*

[155] Weigmann, K. (2013). Elixirs of death. International organizations are working towards a global solution to address the problem of falsified and substandard medicines, but progress stagnated. *EMBO Reports, 14(7), 597–600.*

[156] White Junod, S. (2000). Diethylene glycol deaths in Haiti. *Public Health Reports, 115, 78–86.*

[157] Arie, S. (2012). Contaminated drugs are held responsible for 120 deaths in Pakistan. *BMJ, 344, e951.*

[158] Mintz, C. S., and Liu, J. (2013). China's heparin revisited: What went wrong and has anything Changed. *Journal of Commercial Biotechnology, 19(1).*

[159] Institute of Medicine [IOM]. (2013). Countering the problem of falsified and substandard drugs. Washington, DC: The National Academies Press.

[160] Addis Ababa Declaration on Combating Pharmaceutical Crime. 12 December 2013. at http://www.interpol.int/News-and-media/News/2013/N20131216.

[161] Pan-American Network [PAN] for Drug Regulation Harmonization Anti-Counterfeiting Group. *WHO Drug Information, 2008, 22(4), 278.*

[162] Pandya, S. K. (1988). Letter from Bombay—An unmitigated tragedy. *BMJ, 297, 117–119.*

[163] Penn, R. G. (1979). The state control of medicines: the first 3000 years. *British Journal of Clinical Pharmacology, 8, 293–305.*

[164] Bates et al. (2011). The danger of substandard drugs in emerging markets: an assessment of basic quality. *Pharmacologia, 3(2), 46–51.*

[165] Bassat, Q., Tanner, M., Guerin, P. J., Stricker, K., and Hamed, K. (2016). Combating poor-quality anti-malarial medicines: call to action. *Malaria Journal, 15, 302.*

[166] Fadlallah, R., El-Jardali, F., Annan, F., Azzam, H., and Akl, E. A. (2016). Strategies and Systems-Level Interventions to Combat or Prevent Drug Counterfeiting: A Systematic Review of Evidence Beyond Effectiveness. *Pharmaceutical Medicine, 30(5), 263–276.*

Section 2

Regional Specific Issues of International Trade

Chapter 4

Brazil in the Twenty-First-Century International Trade: Challenges and Opportunities

Susan Elizabeth Martins Cesar de Oliveira

Additional information is available at the end of the chapter

http://dx.doi.org/10.5772/66259

Abstract

This chapter discusses the impacts of globalization on international trade patterns and the required shifts in trade policies. Highlighting the effects of production fragmentation, geographic dispersion and the expansion of global value chains (GVCs), the chapter outlines the Brazilian experience to illustrate the difficulties that various countries face in acknowledging this economic reality and providing appropriate policy responses. It draws on the global value chains literature to analyze Brazil's foreign trade policies implemented during the recent ruling of the Labor Party (PT) presidents Lula da Silva and Dilma Rousseff (2003 to 2015), discussing the Brazilian strategy (or the lack of one) to integrate into global value chains. Results of this exercise have led to the conclusion that a non–GVC-oriented trade policy has allowed Brazil to integrate only superficially into globalized international production and commercial flows. The chapter concludes providing an outlook on the policy shifts required for increasing Brazil's insertion into global value chains and boosting a more prominent role in international trade.

Keywords: Brazil, foreign trade, global value chains, trade policy, globalization

1. Introduction

The beginning of the twenty-first century has witnessed many shifts in international trade patterns and its composition, resulting from the evolution in the economic globalization process. Under the logic of transnational companies, the objectives of cross-border trading have become wider and more complex. Production fragmentation in tasks and its geographic dispersion in global value chains (GVCs) have fostered a multilayered relational framework linking international trade, support services to the companies' core activities and foreign direct investment.

This rapidly evolving scenario has generated important implications for trade policy. It has different meanings depending on each country's domestic context. Developed nations, for instance, are concerned about retaining jobs and keeping the upper-level activities in the value chain. Some developing economies, on the other hand, are proactively making efforts to engage in global value chains, while for other countries the main concerns are linked to upgrading in value chains.

Policy responses to these challenges have been different around the globe. A number of countries have effectively implemented trade policies informed by the GVC's framework, focusing on promoting export competitiveness, attracting investments and supporting the internationalization of their businesses. On the other hand, the debate over GVCs and the new trade patterns is still in early stages in some nations, which have failed to recognize the deep changes in the international trade structure. Currently, a protectionist movement has also gained momentum, opposing globalization and geared towards slowing the pace of international economic integration.

In light of this context, this chapter is aimed at discussing the Brazilian strategy (or the lack of one) to integrate into global value chains and reap the benefits of a stronger participation in international trade. It focuses on the Brazilian experience, centering its analysis on the foreign trade policy responses this important emerging economy has implemented in the last 13 years of the Labor Party's (PT) government (2003–2015). The chapter draws on the GVC's literature to provide a comprehensive landscape of Brazil's foreign trade policies, analyzing primary trade data (traditional and value added) and building a qualitative discussion of government development plans, trade and investment regulations and policies.

The chapter comprises three sections. The first section discusses the "twenty-first-century trade" features. The second section outlines the current level of Brazilian participation in global value chains (GVCs). The third section presents the concept of a "GVCs-oriented trade policy," encompassing four variables, which are tested against Brazil's empirical experience. The conclusion brings an outlook on the political shifts required for increasing Brazil's insertion into global value chains and boosting a more prominent role in international trade.

2. International trade in the twenty-first century

International trade has undergone profound shifts, playing a central role in the production process of companies now organized in global value chains (GVCs). In a deeply connected world, where companies rely on cross-border flows for "making goods" instead of just "selling goods" [1], international trade is no longer limited to the traditional sale of a final good "made in" a country to consumers in another region. The development of global value chains evolved in parallel to economic globalization and both processes have had common catalysts: new information and communication technologies, reduction in transportation costs and trade and investment liberalization.

http://dx.doi.org/10.5772/66259

International trade in goods has increased from approximately US$ 10 trillion in 2004 to US $ 18.5 trillion in 2014, while world trade in services has risen from US$ 2 trillion to nearly US $ 5 trillion in the same period [2]. The increase in international trade in intermediate inputs and components, which accounted for almost US$ 8 trillion in 2014, illustrates the production fragmentation, its geographic dispersion and the complexity of current production systems, with multilayered international sourcing networks.

The concept of global value chains has been used to characterize the set of activities that companies and workers perform in the process of developing a product, from its conception to end use, and also including after-sale services [3]. Under this concept, the usual stages in a production chain are included: inputs; research and development; manufacture; distribution; marketing; and after-sales services. These activities have increasingly become fragmented and geographically dispersed around the globe. The functional integration of these tangible and intangible value-adding activities or tasks and its governance is a key feature of this concept, differentiating trade within global value chains from traditional arm's-length trade [4].

Linked to the evolution of global value chains, the concept of "trade in tasks" emerged to illustrate that each stage of value adding to a good, throughout its production chain process, can be seen as a task with potential to be internationally transacted inter- or intracompanies [5]. The cross-border trade of tasks is aimed at minimizing production and transaction costs and achieving gains in competitiveness. Following this private sector logic, countries may now specialize in certain tasks rather than in productive sectors or complete value chains.

This increasing fragmentation of production stages and its dispersion around the globe has highlighted the complexity of the nexus among trade, investments, services and intellectual property [6]. The concept of "twenty-first-century international trade" reflects these multiples linkages in the transactions within global value chains. In order to understand the current trade patterns, it is required a joint analysis of these intertwined factors: (i) trade in goods, mainly parts and components; (ii) international investments in production plants, training, technology and long-term business relationships; (iii) the use of infrastructure services (telecommunications, internet, parcel delivery, air transport, etc.) to coordinate the production; and (iv) international flows of knowledge, intellectual property and tacit exchanges of know-how. The concept of "twenty-first-century trade" reflects, in sum, the implications of trade globalization and its deep linkages with finance and productive globalization.

The international trade landscape has also changed due to the increased South-South trade and the proliferation of preferential trade agreements. Between 1948 and 1994, the General Agreement on Tariffs and Trade (GATT) received 124 notifications of regional trade agreements (covering trade in goods). Since the establishment of the World Trade Organization (WTO) in 1995, the number of agreements in force increased to 267 [7]. Currently, all WTO members have at least one regional trade agreement in force. Multilateral trade agreements, however, have not advanced in the same pace. The WTO Doha Round, launched in 2001, has not been concluded and members have signed only a trade facilitation agreement.

3. Brazil's insertion in global value chains and world trade

During the 2000s, Brazil raised in the international scene as a promising emerging economy, showcasing a widely praised "growth-with-social-inclusion" model that leveraged the country to the seventh position in the global GDP rank. Brazil's emergence, however, has been much more linked to the triad "credit, domestic consumption and commodities" rather than the development of a world-class industry, leading global value chains and capable of placing Brazil ahead of the international competition.

In 2014, Brazil accounted for only 1.2% of the global exports of goods, ranking 25th in the top exporters rank. Brazil exported US$ 225 billion, and imported US$ 239 billion [8]. Brazil's participation in global services trade is also small. In 2014, Brazil exported US$ 40 billion in commercial services, while imported US$ 87 billion. Low linkages to global value chains, as well as decreasing industrial labor productivity, poor innovation rates and an obsolete industrial park have hampered the growth of Brazil's participation in world trade.

Among the top 25 exporters, Brazil ranks 24th in terms of participation in GVCs, with a 37% rate of integration [9]. Brazil's integration level, Brazil's integration level is slightly higher than India's (36%), but lower than China's (59%), Russia (56%) and South Africa (59%). The ratio of domestic value-added content in Brazilian gross exports is significantly high, exceeding 90%, the second highest among G20 countries [10]. This figure reflects Brazil's role as supplier of raw materials and primary inputs for GVCs. This high level of domestic value added would be positive if reflecting industrial production. However, in the Brazilian case, it is mainly the result of high share of primary goods and commodities in exports. In 2015, for instance, the agribusiness sector accounted for more than 46% of Brazil's total exports [11].

OECD-WTO Trade in Value Added (TiVA) database's figures released in 2015, which measured trade in valued added for year 2011, have confirmed Brazil's low engagement in GVCs. In 2011, ICT and electronics industry had the highest foreign value added share in Brazil's exports, accounting for 24.1%, followed by coke and petroleum (21.4%) and motor vehicles (19.9%). OECD-WTO TiVA analysis have also highlighted the underdevelopment of a regional value chain in Latin America, contrasting with the linkages found in North America, Europe and East Asia. Brazil's major import and export markets are from outside the region. In 2011, China directly imported one-quarter of all Brazil's intermediate exports in value-added terms [12].

Brazil's low participation in international trade reflects the inward orientation of its development strategy implemented along the 13 years (2003–2015) that the PT (Labour Party) governed Brazil. During this period, three versions of industrial policies have been launched, using traditional "picking winners" strategies, strong local content requirements and the goal of developing and maintaining full production chains within the country.

In 2003, early in the first term of former President Lula da Silva, the government launched the Industrial, Technological and Foreign Trade Policy (PITCE), aimed at promoting gains in competitiveness through technological innovation [13]. PITCE focused on technology intensive sectors, such as capital goods, semiconductors, biotechnology and software. The

http://dx.doi.org/10.5772/66259

government considered these sectors as key to develop Brazil's innovation system and to transfer productivity gains to the rest of the industry.

Five years later, the government revamped this policy, launching in 2008 the Productive Development Policy (PDP). This policy provided a detailed roadmap for actions in 25 sectors, aimed at upgrading the industrial pattern of investments. Due to the international economic crisis in 2008 and 2009, however, this policy became a set of anti-cyclical measures rather than initiatives capable of structurally transforming the industrial sector.

The "Greater Brazil Plan" (Plano Brasil Maior), launched in 2011 in the first term of President Dilma Rousseff, was the last broad industrial policy implemented in Brazil, focusing on promoting technologic and production competencies to strengthen domestic value chains [14]. One of the core guidelines of the plan was to promote a "structural change in Brazil's insertion into the international economy." It was aimed at diversifying and boosting exports, seeking to increase Brazil's share in international trade from 1.36% in 2010 to 1.60% in 2014. Trade-related policies focused on the following objectives: (a) promoting exports of intermediate-technology and knowledge-intensive products, (b) supporting the internationalization of companies through product differentiation and greater domestic value added, and (c) rooting foreign companies in Brazil and attracting research and development (R & D) centers.

Although these industrial policies suggested a roadmap for fostering national competitiveness, they still did not reflect a full understanding of the structural changes in the global production system, increasingly internationally dispersed and fragmented in GVCs. The empirical results of PITCE, PDP and Greater Brazil Plan have been criticized because international trade and industrial activity indicators for the period point to a specialization in low-technology goods and commodities.

In spite of the governmental efforts to foster innovation and increase technological content in exports, Brazil consolidated a position of commodities exporter. The share of non-manufactured exports increased from 19.9% in 2003 to 37.7% in 2015. Furthermore, the share of exports of high-technology products decreased from 7% in 2003 to 5.2% in 2015, and the share of medium-high technology exports decreased from 22.8 to 16 % in the same period. On the other hand, the profile of imports remained relatively stable, with medium-high technology products accounting for 42.7% of the total Brazilian imports in 2015. Likewise, the analysis of the technological intensity of Brazil's trade balance shows an increased trade deficit in high and medium-high technology goods. In 2015, Brazil had a US $ 22.8 billion trade deficit in high-technology products and a US $ 42.7 billion deficit in medium-high technology products [15].

During the first mandate of the Dilma Rousseff administration (2011–2014), furthermore, Brazilian foreign trade flows of goods showed a decrease, from US $ 482.3 billion in 2011 to US $ 454.1 in 2014. Commercial services' trade had just a slight increase. In 2011, Brazil exported US $ 37.11 billion, while imported US $ 73.1 billion. In 2014, Brazil exported US $ 39 billion and imported US $ 85.9 billion [16].

Rousseff's economic policy departed from the three pillars maintained in the previous government (primary surplus, floating exchange rate and inflation targets), and Brazil's economic fundamentals started to deteriorate. Brazilian trade followed the downward trend. Exports declined from a 2011 peak of US $ 256 billion to US $ 191.1 billion in 2015. In 2015 (the first year of Rouseff's second term), trade flows continued to drop, decreasing to US $ 362.5 billion, while Brazil's GDP contracted 3.8% and trade accounted for only 27% of the GDP [17]. Combined with a large corruption scandal, the economic recession led to Rouseff's impeachment in 2016.

4. GVC-prone foreign trade policies: Brazil's profile

GVC-oriented trade policies can positively influence the integration of domestic enterprises into the world economy, as well as attracting and retaining high value-added activities into the country. In a world of global value chains, an integration prone foreign trade policy includes four variables [18]: (i) adoption of an updated concept of international trade, recognizing the nexus among trade of final goods, intermediates, services, investment and intellectual property flows; (ii) focus on facilitating market access to inputs and intermediary goods into the domestic market and seeks preferential access for exports into key foreign markets; (iii) recognizes heterodox trade barriers, such as infrastructure, support services, business environment, among others; and (iv) foreign trade promotion targets the integration of small and medium enterprises into global value chains.

Since the early 2000s, however, Brazil has not followed this GVC-oriented model. Instead, the Brazilian foreign trade policy has been crafted under the umbrella of larger industrial development plans, explained in the previous section. The government has favored the development of full production chains within the country instead of specializing and integrating into global value chains.

Looking at the first recommendation of the model, "adoption of an updated definition of international trade," Brazilian policies have only partially recognized the trade-investment-intellectual property nexus. Although the policies have taken into account the connection between trade and investments, it is not clear the recognition of the importance of imports of world-class inputs and parts for improving exports competitiveness. Brazil's understanding of the integrated trade concept, furthermore, seems to be limited, not including components connected to intellectual property, information and innovation flows among countries. In the diplomatic practice, an example of this disconnection can be observed in the science, technology and innovation agreements, since these partnerships are not perceived as potential elements for foreign trade policy.

During the Lula da Silva two terms (2003–2010), the President himself engaged in commercial diplomacy initiatives, strongly promoting the establishment of a "new international trade geography," pursuing a diversification of Brazilian commercial partnerships, focusing on a larger relationship with countries of the South. Brazil also prioritized relations with MERCOSUR, seeking to deepen the regional integration and the creation of a space for expanded cooperation in South America.

http://dx.doi.org/10.5772/66259

It is important to note that in that period, however, the search for new business partnerships was not linked to a viewpoint of improving the integration of domestic firms into global production chains. The mainstream perception regarding the international trade structure was still related to the traditional North-South cleavage, and the rapprochement to developing countries was a general orientation of the Brazilian foreign policy in the period. Brazil's search for a more prominent role in foreign trade faded in Dilma Rousseff's term, in face of other government priorities and the low prestige granted to foreign policy issues in the period.

Taking into account the "market access" aspect of a GVC-oriented trade policy, Brazil's approach has favored protection, instead of liberalization. Governmental actions in this direction have included tariff increases, nontariff barriers and strengthening of trade remedy mechanisms. Furthermore, Brazil continues to have a high level of tariff protection through MERCOSUR's Common External Tariff, which averages 14.1% applied rate for non-agricultural goods and 10.2% for agricultural goods [19].

Brazilian trade policy has emphasized the implementation of trade remedy measures, beginning with the introduction of a "New Strategy of the Brazilian Trade Remedies System," in 2003. More recently, the government has increased the number of personnel dedicated to this issue at the Ministry of Development, Industry and Foreign Trade. Brazil applied 112 definitive trade remedy measures from 2003 to 2010 and 152 measures from 2011 to 2015. These numbers have significantly increased compared to the eight years before the Lula da Silva government, when 66 definitive measures had been applied, including antidumping and safeguards [20].

During the 2003–2010 period, Brazil engaged in large market access initiatives that could not be concluded. At the beginning of the first term of President Lula, two parallel negotiations were at the top of the government agenda: the Free Trade Area of the Americas (FTAA) and the MERCOSUR-European Union (EU) negotiations. Such agreements would be instrumental in increasing Brazil's insertion in global value chains, taking into account that the United States and the European Union are dynamic centers in various industries that could leverage Brazil's participation in global and regional production networks.

Negotiations of the FTAA, however, were suspended in 2005, due to irreconcilable differences between Brazil's and the USA's negotiating approach and also regarding the scope of the agreement. Brazilian interests to maintain "policy space" to implement its industrial policies prevailed against offensive interests of part of the industry and the agribusiness sector. In parallel, the MERCOSUR-European Union negotiation, which in a way had been driven by the prospect of competition that would be generated by the conclusion of the FTAA, lost momentum in the following years. Negotiations resumed in 2010 and had relatively small progress to date.

In spite of these two large regional free trade initiatives, Brazil's top priority continued to be the Doha Development Round of multilateral trade negotiations. The Brazilian government believed this to be the ideal forum to address key trade issues, such as greater market access for agricultural products in developed countries and subsidies reduction. Taking into account the deadlock in the Round, there was little progress in terms of greater market access for Brazilian companies from 2003 to 2015. Brazil/MERCOSUR concluded extra-regional free trade agreements only with Israel (2007), Egypt (2010) and Palestine (2011). The FTA with Israel is the only one currently in force, the others still need to be ratified. MERCOSUR also signed limited preferential trade agreements with India (2004) and the South African Customs Union—SACU (2009). In all these agreements, liberalization applies only to goods, not including services or investments, which are core issues under the global value chains framework.

Regarding the negotiation of foreign investment protection agreements, Brazil remained dormant during a long period. Although in the early 1990s Brazil had signed 14 FIPAs that contained investor-state clauses, this model was considered inconsistent with the Brazilian constitution and the agreements never entered into force. The increase in the number of Brazilian companies investing abroad in the 2000s prompted the government to revisit the issue and develop a Brazilian framework for a "cooperation and investment facilitation agreement." Brazil has successfully concluded agreements with Angola, Mozambique, Malawi, Mexico Colombia and Peru. This model has a state-state dispute settlement mechanism, and leaves more space for developing domestic regulations that could be challenged in the traditional FIPAs [21].

In light of the small level of success in the market access negotiations during the 2003–2015 years, the WTO dispute settlement system increased in importance for Brazil's trade strategy. Brazil has been one of the most active participants of the WTO dispute settlement system. Since the establishment of the Dispute Settlement Body in 1995, Brazil has participated in 29 panels as complainant, 16 disputes as respondent and in 102 cases as interested third party [22]. Brazil has won some emblematic "victories" for the domestic exporting sector, such as the dispute with the United States regarding subsidies for cotton production (DS 267), the dispute regarding sugar exports subsidies granted by the European Union (DS 266) and the dispute on the rate of equalization on the USA's imports of orange juice (DS 382).

Taking into account the third aspect of a GVC-oriented trade policy, the Brazilian government has not directly recognized the "heterodox" barriers to trade, such as infrastructure, support services and business environment. Although the government has implemented a large "Growth Acceleration Plan" geared towards transport infrastructure projects, the plan was not focused on exporters' demands. Efforts to reduce red tape and improve Brazil's business environment have not materialized, and the so-called "Brazilian cost" remains as a nontraditional barrier to trade as well as to the attraction of foreign direct investment.

Trade promotion policies—the last element analyzed in the GVC-oriented trade policy model —have been aimed at strengthening the relationship with other developing countries. Between 2003 and 2015, trade promotion efforts resulted in an increase in trade with Africa, Middle East and Asian countries. In this period, China emerged as Brazil's main trade partner, surpassing the United States and absorbing 18.63% of Brazilian global exports in 2015. In contrast, traditional partners like the European Union and the United States have lost importance as a destination for Brazilian exports. In 2003, for instance, 22.8% of Brazilian exports went to the USA and 25.7% to the EU, while, in 2015, this share had decreased to 12.6 and 17.7%, respec-

http://dx.doi.org/10.5772/66259

tively. Exports to MERCOUR remained relatively stable. In 2003, Brazilian exports to the bloc accounted for 7.7% of total exports, while, in 2015, MERCOSUR imported 9.4% of Brazil's total exports.

Brazil has focused in policies for fostering small and medium enterprises' exports. Brazil's Export Promotion Agency (APEX), however, has given greater attention to traditional trade promotion and intelligence tools. Market reports have not focused on production chains, and they have not developed guides or special mechanisms for linking SME with GVC's leader companies. Similarly, the Ministry of Foreign Affairs has not oriented the commercial sections in embassies abroad to proactively seek supply opportunities with leader companies.

5. Conclusion: towards a repositioning in global value chains?

This chapter has argued that in the last 13 years Brazil has not adopted a proactive stance towards a greater engagement into GVCs. Taking into account that greater integration requires trade openness, improved market access, GVC-oriented trade promotion, and an expanded vision of international trade that integrates goods, services, investments and intellectual property, Brazil seems to only superficially commit to globalization. Brazil's shallow integration is in part a result of trade policies aimed at protecting the domestic market and establishing a market reserve for Brazilian companies in MERCOSUR.

Recent research has demonstrated the positive economic outcomes of engaging in global value chains. A GVC-oriented trade policy can positively influence integration of domestic enterprises into GVCs, as well as attracting high value-added activities. In order to achieve the objectives of improving Brazil's competitiveness and promoting a better insertion in the international economy, it would be recommend a reassessment of the policies aimed at protecting the domestic and regional market. In a world where industrial production is fragmented and geographically dispersed, Brazil continues to pursue a vision that it is still possible and desirable to internalize most of the tasks involved in the multiple steps of adding value to a product. It seeks to sell internationally a product totally "made in Brazil," even at the expense of protecting inefficient industries.

Brazil's new government of President Michel Temer (PMDB), which took power after the impeachment of the former President Dilma Rousseff in 2016, has given signs that it will shift the country foreign trade strategy towards greater integration. A revamped trade policy will be constrained, however, by external, domestic and MERCOSUR challenges.

In terms of external constraints, it would be important to highlight the following factors: (i) the delay in recovery of the international economy, (ii) the declining support for multilateral and regional free trade negotiations, (iii) the loss of an important window of opportunity for economic integration agreements (such as the failed FTAA negotiations and delays in negotiations between MERCOSUR and the EU), and (iv) the fact that Brazil is outside the major regional trade liberalization initiatives, such as the Trans-Pacific Partnership (TPP) and other new-generation agreements.

Moreover, economic and commercial globalization in all its complexity acts as a systemic constraint for Brazil's insertion. Although Brazil seeks a new level of participation in international trade, it is reluctant to abandon practices and perceptions that only made sense in a context of international production of the last century. One of the main obstacles to a complete transition to a modern trade policy would be to adopt a more positive stance towards imports of raw materials, intermediate products and components, taking into account their key role in the production of goods for both domestic consumption and for reexporting.

Domestically, the most significant challenges are related to overcoming the historic protectionist orientation and pressures from organized industrial associations. Second, the misperception of the government in the sense that agribusiness and commodities are the main offensive interests in Brazil's trade liberalization negotiations, leaving the domestic industry linked to defensive interests of protection against a possible increase in foreign competition in the domestic market. Finally, additional challenges towards a greater participation in global value chains are linked to issues such as trade facilitation, reduction of red tape and logistics problems caused by deficiencies in trade infrastructure.

Among the challenges arising from Brazil's participation in MERCOSUR, the continuity of the 4+1 negotiating model (i.e., member countries cannot negotiate individually preferential trade agreements) for liberalization agreements with other regions seems to be the most relevant, as this mechanism becomes even more complex with the expansion of the number of MERCOSUR members. Moreover, other challenges include the deepening of the political and economic crisis in Venezuela, and how MERCOSUR will solve the problem of fully integrating the country into the bloc or reverting its accession process that was controversially approved in 2010.

In sum, Brazil has not adopted a GVC-oriented trade policy. This does not mean, however, that it has become an isolated country. Nevertheless, the mainstream mind frame during Lula da Silva's government and Dilma Rouseff's term favored the construction of Brazil's own model for economic development and international insertion, which had a limited level of success. Revamping Brazil's international trade policy will be key for recovering Brazil's economic development path.

Author details

Susan Elizabeth Martins Cesar de Oliveira

Address all correspondence to: susan@unb.br

University of Brasília, Brasília, Brazil

References

[1] Baldwing, R. Multilateralizing 21st-century regionalism. Available at http://voxeu.org/article/multilateralising-21st-century-regionalism

[2] UNCTAD. Key statistics and trends in international trade – 2015. Geneva, 2015. Available at http://unctad.org/en/PublicationsLibrary/ditctab2015d1_en.pdf

[3] Gereffi, G., Fernandez-Stark, K. Global Value Chain Analysis: A Primer. Center on Globalization, Governance and Competitiveness, 2011.

[4] Gereffi, G., Humphrey, J., Sturgeon, T. The governance of global value chains. Review of International Political Economy, 2005.

[5] Grossman, G., Rossi-Hansberg, E. Trading tasks: A simple theory of offshoring. American Economic Review, 98:5, pp. 1978–1997, 2008.

[6] Baldwin, R. Global supply chains: why they emerged, why they matter and where are they going. In: Elms, D.; Low, P. Global Value Chains in a Changing World. Fung Foundation, Temasek Foudation and World Trade Organization, 2013.

[7] World Trade Organization Regional Trade Agreements Database. Available at https://www.wto.org/english/tratop_e/region_e/region_e.htm

[8] World Trade Organization Trade Report, 2015. Available at https://www.wto.org/english/res_e/publications_e/wtr15_e.htm

[9] UNCTAD (Eora GVC Database). Available at http://unctad.org/en/PublicationsLibrary/diae2013d1_en.pdf.

[10] OECD. Interconnected Economies: Benefiting from Global Value Chains, 2013. Available at http://www.oecd.org/industry/ind/stayingcompetitiveintheglobaleconomymovingupthevaluechainsynthesisreport.htm.

[11] Brazilian Ministry of Agriculture Statistics Database (AGROSTAT), 2016. Available at http://indicadores.agricultura.gov.br/agrostat/index.htm

[12] OECD-WTO TiVA database. Brazil country note, 2015. Available at http://www.oecd.org/sti/ind/tiva/CN_2015_Brazil.pdf

[13] ABDI. Agência Brasileira de Desenvolvimento Industrial. Dez anos de política industrial: balanço/perspectivas. Brasília: ABDI, 2015. Available at http://www.abdi.com.br/Estudo/Artigos%20ABDI%20-%20Externo%2024042015.pdf

[14] Câmara dos Deputados. Análise do Plano Brasil Maior. Consultoria Legislativa. Brasília, 2013. Available at http://www2.camara.leg.br/documentos-e-pesquisa/publicacoes/estnottec/areas-da-conle/tema10/2013_7665_versao%20para%20publicacao.pdf

[15] Ministry of Development, Industry and Foreign Trade. Foreign Trade Statistics. Available at http://www.mdic.gov.br/comercio-exterior/estatisticas-de-comercio-exterior

[16] Ministry of Development, Industry and Foreign Trade. Overview of International Trade, 2015. Available at http://www.mdic.gov.br/images/REPOSITORIO/scs/decin/Estat%C3%ADsticas_de_Com%C3%A9rcio_Exterior/2015/Panorama_Oficial_2015_-_Com_Capa.pdf

[17] World Bank National Accounts Data. Trade (% of GDP). Available at http://data.worldbank.org/indicator/NE.TRD.GNFS.ZS

[18] de Oliveira, S. E. M. C. Cadeias Globais de Valor e os novos padrões de comércio internacional. Brasília: FUNAG, 2015. Available at http://funag.gov.br/loja/index.php?route=product/product&product_id=743

[19] WTO. Brazil's tariff profile. Available at http://stat.wto.org/TariffProfiles/BR_e.htm

[20] Ministry of Development, Industry and Foreign Trade. Trade Remedies Report. Various years. Available at http://www.mdic.gov.br/comercio-exterior/defesa-comercial/853-relatorios-de-defesa-comercial

[21] Apex-Brasil. Acordos de facilitação e promoção de investimentos: uma nova abordagem para a promoção de investimentos brasileiros na África. Boletim de Facilitação de Negócios. Ano 2- Junho de 2015. Edição 3. Available at http://arq.apexbrasil.com.br/portal/BoletimNegocios_Edicao03.pdf

[22] WTO. Disputes by Country/Territory. Brazil, 2016. Available at https://www.wto.org/english/tratop_e/dispu_e/dispu_by_country_e.htm

Chapter 5

Malaysia and China: The Trade Balances, Foreign Exchanges and Crises Impacts

Tze-Haw Chan

Additional information is available at the end of the chapter

http://dx.doi.org/10.5772/66977

Abstract

China appears as the biggest trading partner for ASEAN economies, but it is inconclusive whether the complementarities between China and regional economies offset China's competitive threat. This study tries to assess if real exchange fluctuations and the demand-supply channels determine the Malaysia-China trade balances in the global crises era, 1997–2010. The finding generally supports the complementary role of China in the Malaysia-China bilateral trading. However, despite the long-run effect of real exchange on trade balances, the Keynesian demand channel was not uphold during and after the global financial crisis—due to the contractionary effect on Malaysian output. The Chinese inflation impact is also not evident following the foreign exchange shocks. Meanwhile, currency devaluation for exports gains is insufficient to sustain Malaysia output expansion against China. Further productivity growth in real and tradable sectors is essentially needed.

Keywords: trade balances, contractionary effect, global crises, VARX, VECMX

1. Introduction

China has become the largest trading partner for many of the East Asian nations in the aftermath of Asian financial crisis 1997/1998. For Southeast Nations (ASEAN-10), China accounted for 12.9% of the regional trade, surpassing the USA (8.1%) and Japan (10.6%) in 2012. The figure was only about 2.2 and 1.9%, respectively, for total exports and imports of ASEAN-China, a decade ago (ASEAN Statistical Yearbook). A number of recent studies have thus documented the complementary effects of China for its trading neighbors in line with the improved economic link [1–4]. Multinational corporations are incorporating China into the global production system along with earlier entrants and hence promoting regional trading [5]. China's own enterprises are specializing, in coordination with regional counterparts, and so raising intraindustry trade in differentiated products. In other words, the emergence of China as a global economic power has resulted in an increase of labor diversification and intraregional trading, which, in the long run, may lead to regional economic integration similar to the European Union or the North American Free Trade Agreement [6, 7].

Yet, others have also pointed out the conflicting (competing) features of China's economic rise. China appeared as the world's leading exporter since 2007, and its current account surplus amounted to about $260 billion (Ministry of Commerce, China),[1] which ranked top globally in 2013. There are worries that China's yuan regime, investment magnetism, and low labor costs, as well as its accession to the World Trade Organization (November 2001), may have positioned the country as a formidable economic competitor that threatens to crowd out other developing Asian countries [5, 8–10]. Malaysia, for instance, has suffered a continuous seven-year trade deficit with China since 2002—which peaked at $4.2 billion in 2007, before the major correction in 2009. Some observers have also, directly or indirectly, related the resurgence of China since the late 1980s and the devaluation of the renminbi (or, Chinese yuan) in 1994 to the Asia financial crisis[2] [11, 12]. Such issues have gravely challenged the consensus of sustainable trade competitiveness at the regional level. Up to now, no conclusive consensus has been reached concerning the economic emergence of China. It is still difficult to assess whether the complementarities between China and regional economies offset its competitive threat [5, 13–15].

This study focuses on the Malaysia-China case to assess if the real exchange fluctuations as well as the demand and supply channels determine the performance of bilateral trade balances in the global crises era, 1997–2010. Among the ASEAN-10 members, Malaysia is presently the largest trading partner with China. In 2009, the Malaysia-China trade reached $59 billion—about 18.9% of Malaysia's global trading, surpassing the Malaysia-US trade share (10.9%). The figure for Malaysia-China trade was only $4.7 billion in 1990 or about 8% of Malaysian total trade.

To the best of our knowledge, previous studies have worked on the Malaysian or the Chinese case but not for Malaysia vis-à-vis China after the major adjustment of yuan and ringgit in July 2005. Likewise, no updated studies have assessed the period of postsubprime crisis.[3] Yet, it was noted in the literature that time period of the study being selected would have resulted in dissimilar results. Malaysia, for instance, has practiced various exchange rate regimes in the past four decades—the Bretton Woods system, managed floating, free floating, and basket of currency-floating eras. Different regimes have reflected varied policy responses, and

[1] Available at http://english.mofcom.gov.cn/article/statistic/BriefStatistics/201401/20140100466521.shtml

[2] The fall of the renminbi implied a real exchange rate appreciation for the dollar-pegged currencies in East Asia, which their fragile financial systems were unable to absorb. Some of them were thrown into prolonged current account deficits and forced to devalue their currencies in order to regain their export market share, which eventually led to the Asia financial crisis in 1997.

[3] For example, Baharumshah [16] studied cases of Malaysia-US-Japan and Thailand-US-Japan for the period of 1980Q1–1996Q4; Ahmad and Yang [17] studied China against G7 during 1974–1994; Bahmani-Oskooee and Harvey [18, 19] studied Malaysia vis-à-vis 14 trading partners for 1983Q1–2002Q1 and 1973Q1–2001Q3, respectively; Bahmani-Oskooee and Wang [20] then studied China and 13 major trading partners during 1983–2002, but without Malaysia.

http://dx.doi.org/10.5772/66977

the empirical results could be irreconcilable with the theoretical prediction, over time. As for China, the open policy started in 1978, but the progress of trade and exchange rate liberalization was slow prior to the 1990s. Both nations, however, share a similar exchange rate regime since 1998. Though claimed as managed float by the Chinese authority, Chinese yuan was *de facto* pegged to the USD at RMB8.28 from 1998 through June 2005 [21]. Malaysia, on the other hand, was officially pegged to US$ at RM3.80 in a similar period. By July 2005, Chinese yuan was appreciated against the US$ while Malaysian ringgit de-pegged from the US$. Our study thus considers only 1997–2010, a period of economic liberalization and trade expansion for both China and Malaysia, where potential structural breaks due to global and regional crises are taken into accounts.

The study contributes to expand the literature by taking concerns of several distinguished empirical issues. First, instead of measuring the trade balance as a function of the real exchange rate, domestic income and foreign income in the conventional way, we also incorporate domestic and foreign prices in our empirical model. The consideration emphasizes on the China's role in the supply and value chain of Malaysian economics and the assessment of potential imported inflation effect (or, deflation), which is of important issue to stabilize domestic economy.

Second, Malaysia is a small and open economy, with the exchange rate regime playing an important role in economic development. When compared to the Chinese population of 1.35 billion people with GDP (at PPP) amounted to US$11,347 billion, the Malaysian market size is relatively small, with only 28 million residents and GDP (at PPP) of US$464 billion. Though Malaysian trade openness is now among the highest in the world (about 200% of its GDP), its total trade volume is relatively still small. It is necessary, in the methodological sense, to develop an econometric model that allows the possibility of drawing a distinction between endogenous and exogenous variables, which are integrated of $I(1)$. This chapter employs the VARX and VECMX modeling procedures put advanced by Pesaran et al. [22], which further applied by Garatt et al. [23, 24] and Assenmacher-Wesche and Pesaran [25], to construct a cointegrating VARX in the presence of $I(1)$ exogenous or long-run forcing variables (which, in our case, the Chinese variables). A reduced-form error correction of the VECMX model can then be estimated, where variables are separated into the conditional model and marginal model, respectively. This approach allows us to impose long-run relationships and short-run dynamic restrictions based on economic theory.

In addition, the compilation and analysis of macroeconomic data of both nations by previous studies are also limited by the unavailability of higher frequency series—monthly data. We, therefore, focus on the post-liberalization period (January 1997 to March 2010) where both Malaysian and Chinese series are more valid and reliable. We reconstruct the series that sourced from Datastream, in consider of the seasonal and based-year effects. Our data are also cross-checked with the GVAR database provided by Smith and Galesi [26]. Then we conduct a preliminary test of endogenous break(s)[4] on each series and impose the break dates as dummy variables in the VARX and VECMX models.

[4]To determine the potential endogenous break(s), we follow the structural break tests of Saikkonen and Lütkepohl [27].

What follows involves the estimation issue for small sample size, particularly, in regard to the size and power properties of time series analysis. Though with 159 monthly observations, our study only covers a 13-year length of time. Given this, we employ the nonparametric bootstrap method, an alternative to the large sample data tests based on asymptotic theory. It was well noted in the literature that bootstrap's ability to provide asymptotic refinements often leads to a reduction of size distortions in finite sample bias and it generally yields consistent estimators and test statistics [28, 29]. This method is later applied to test the number of VARX cointegrating ranks and to test the significance of log-likelihood ratio (LR) statistics of the overidentifying long-run restrictions. This method is also applied in the measures of estimation uncertainty and confidence intervals for generalized IRF and persistent profile.

Our study reveals that, despite the long-run effect of real exchange on trade balances, the Keynesian demand channel was not uphold during and after the Asia financial crisis—due to the contractionary effect on Malaysian output. Though a potential depreciation of the Malaysian ringgit would have resulted in an overall surplus for Malaysia against China, the domestic and foreign income variables are only significant through lagged effects in the short run but not in the long-run model, suggesting that the demand side effects are temporal. In other words, ringgit devaluation for exports gains is insufficient to sustain output expansion for Malaysia against China. Further productivity growth in real and tradable sectors is essentially needed. On the other hand, the inflation impact is not evidently observed following the foreign exchange shock, implying that China has yet to be Malaysia's main source of imported inflation. Meanwhile, the dummy of subprime crisis is excluded from the trade balance model as insignificant statistic was reported during the restriction test. Having the empirical facts being considered, our study generally supports the complementary role of China in the Malaysia-China bilateral trading.

To this end, our study is designed in the following manner. Section 2 shows the theoretical representation of the trade-exchange rate-output-price model that forms the basis of our empirical model. This is followed by the estimation procedures and data description. Estimation results are discussed in Section 3. Finally, in Section 4, conclusion and policy implications are drawn.

2. Research methodology

The present study takes as a point of departure the standard trade model, variants of which are employed in the literature by Shirvani and Wilbratte [30] and Kandil and Mirzaie [31].

2.1. Trade-exchange rate-output-price model

The model expresses the trade balance as a function of the real exchange rate and the levels of domestic and foreign incomes. Taking the natural logarithm of both sides, we have the following model, with a stochastic term added to capture short-term departures from long-run equilibrium:

$$\ln\left(TB_t\right) = \alpha_0 + \alpha_1 \ln\left(Y_t\right) + \alpha_2 \ln(Y_t^*) + \alpha_3 \ln\left(Q_t\right) + \mu_t \tag{1}$$

where ln represents the natural logarithm and μ is a white process. Note that expressing the trade balance as the ratio of exports to imports allows all variables to be expressed in log form and obviates the need for an appropriate price index to perform our basic statistical tests. However, given that China plays an important role in the supply chain of Malaysian economics, it is important to include the producer prices of both nations. Such consideration is vital to investigate the potential imported inflation or deflation effect following economic shocks. If the domestic and foreign prices are indeed nonconstant and integrated of $I(1)$, the assessment of the price effects is possible. Then, Eq. (1) can be represented by

$$\ln\left(TB_t\right) = \alpha_0 + \alpha_1 \ln\left(Y_t\right) + \alpha_2 \ln(Y_t^*) + \alpha_3 \ln\left(Q_t\right) + \alpha_4 \ln\left(PP_t\right) + \alpha_5 \ln\left(PP_t^*\right) + \mu_t \tag{2}$$

where TB is a unit-free measure of the trade balance, which is defined as the ratio of Malaysian exports to imports vis-à-vis China, Q is defined as the real Malaysian Ringgit, and PP and PP^* are the domestic and foreign producer prices, respectively. If the Marshall-Lerner condition holds, then $\alpha_3 > 1$ so that a real devaluation of domestic currency (RM) improves the trade balance of Malaysia-China trades. Conventionally, real domestic income will be negatively signed ($\alpha_1 < 0$) as an increase in Malaysian income is expected to increase its imports of commodity j, and TB deteriorates. Real foreign income is to be positively signed ($\alpha_2 > 0$) because an increase in Chinese income implies more demand for Malaysian exports and hence TB improves. However, if a rise in Malaysian income is due to an increase in the production of substitute goods for j, the estimate of α_1 could be positive. In the same way, the estimate of α_2 could be also positive or negative [20]. In addition, we assume that changes of producer prices are reflected in import and export prices. A rise in the domestic producer price hampers export competitiveness, and so $\alpha_4 < 0$. Then, $\alpha_5 > 0$ because an increase in the foreign producer price will cause imports to be more expensive and reduce the demand for imports.

2.2. The VARX and VECMX estimation

Pesaran et al. [22] modified and generalized the approach to the problem of estimation and hypothesis testing in the context of the augmented vector error correction model. Garratt et al. [23, 24] extended the idea and developed the VECMX model along the same lines. They distinguish between an $m_y \times 1$ vector of endogenous variables y_t and an $m_x \times 1$ vector of exogenous $I(1)$ variables x_t among the core variables in $z_t = (y'_t, x'_t)$ with $m = m_y + m_x$. Since our sample period consists of the Asia financial crisis, the dot-com bubble, and the global subprime crisis, structural break(s) are necessarily included in the model. Depending on the number of crisis detected by the break tests of Lumsdaine and Papell [32] and Saikkonen and Lütkepohl [27], we impose the shift dummy variable ($D_{crisis,t}$) and the impulse dummy variable ($\Delta D_{crisis,t}$), where $\Delta D_{crisis,t} = D_{crisis,t} - D_{crisis,t-1}$. The former captures the shift in the long-run relations, whereas the latter applies for the short-run dynamic models. The VECMX is then given by

$$\Delta y_t = -\Pi_y Z_{y-1} + {}^\wedge\Delta X_t + \textstyle\sum_{i=1}^{p-1} \psi_i Z_{t-i} + C_0 + C_1 t + C_2 D_{crisis,t} + V_t \tag{3}$$

$$\Delta X_t = \textstyle\sum_{i=1}^{p-1} \Gamma_{xi} \Delta Z_{t-i} + C_{x0} + u_t \tag{4}$$

where there are r cointegrating relation(s) among the 6×1 vector of variables z_t in the conditional model (Eq. (3)) contains four endogenous (Malaysia) variables, $y_t = \{TB_t, Y_t, Q_t, P_t\}$ and the marginal model (Eq. (4)) with two weakly exogenous foreign (China) variables, $x_t = \{Y_t^*, P_t^*\}$. $\Pi_y = \alpha_y \beta'$, α_y is an $(m_y \times r)$ matrix of error correction coefficients and β' is an $(m_y \times r)$ matrix of long-run coefficients and Ψ_i and Λ are the short-run parameters, t is time trend, c_0 is the intercept, and p is the order of VECMX. In the marginal model, Γ_{xi} are the short-run parameters and c_{xo} is the intercept. It is assumed that u_t and v_t are serially uncorrelated and normally distributed. Notice that we need to restrict the trend coefficients in Eq. (3) in order to avoid the quadratic trends and the cumulative effects of $D_{crisis,t}$ in the level solution [22], as follow:

$$c_1 = \Pi_y d_1, c_2 = \Pi_y d_2 \tag{5}$$

where c_1 and c_2 are an arbitrary $(m_y \times 1)$ vector of fixed constants. Note that d_1 and d_2 are unrestricted if Π_y is full rank; in that case $d_1 = \Pi_y^{-1} c_1$ and $d_2 = \Pi_y^{-1} c_2$. However, if Π_y is rank deficient, d_1 and d_2 cannot be fully identified from c_1 and c_2 but can be estimated from the reduced form coefficients. In this case, the reduced form trend coefficients are restricted.

2.3. Data description

The analyses are all based on monthly series, spanning from January 1997 to March 2010. Real exchange rates (Q) are compiled by having the nominal RM/yuan adjusted for relative price changes using consumer price indexes (CPI), whereas trade balance (TB) ratios are computed based on the export/import series. Since monthly observations of GDP are not available, domestic and foreign incomes (Y, Y^*) are proxy by the industrial production index (IPI). The aggregate trade series are sourced from the Direction of Trade Statistics compiled by the International Monetary Fund, whereas the CPI, IPI, producer price indexes, and foreign exchange series are sourced from the DataStream. Our data are being cross-checked with the GVAR database prepared by Smith and Galesi [26] and research team members (Gang Zhang, Ambrogio Cesa Bianchi, and Alessandro Rebucci) at the Inter-American Development Bank.

3. Empirical discussion

The preliminary examination of the data properties is conducted using the unit root tests by Lumsdaine and Papell [32] and Saikkonen and Lütkepohl [27]. The data are overwhelmingly integrated of $I(1)$ where unit roots are rejected at first difference. These tests allow for endogenous structural break(s); for most cases, the break dates fall on the Asian financial crisis and subprime crisis periods.[5] We thereby impose two dummy variables on the trade model.

3.1. Dynamic long-run relationship and error correction modeling

Before proceeding to the cointegration test of long-run relationship, we first have to determine the lag orders of endogenous and exogenous variables outlined in Eq. (3). For this purpose,

[5]Results of unit root tests are not presented here but are available upon request.

http://dx.doi.org/10.5772/66977

the Akaike information criterion (AIC) and the Schwarz Bayesian criterion (SBC) are applied to the underlying unrestricted VARX model. SBC has selected the lag orders of 3 for both conditional and marginal models, whereas AIC selected a higher and same order lag for the endogenous (4) and exogenous (3) variables, respectively. According to Garratt et al. [23] and Affandi [33], underestimating the lag orders is generally more serious than overestimating them. As such, the subsequent analyses are based on the VARX (4, 3).

Next, we need to determine the number of cointegrating relations given by $r = \text{rank}(\Pi_y)$, as defined by Eq (3). Following Pesaran et al. [22], the modified Johansen and Juselius [34] cointegration test is conducted using trace statistics for a model with weakly exogenous regressors. The test results are reported in **Table 1**. It appears that the trace statistics suggests the presence of one cointegrating relation ($r = 1$) at 10% significant level, which is in line with the trade theory expectation.

H_0	H_1	Trace statistics	Bootstrapped critical values	
			95%	90%
$r = 0$	$r = 1$	86.92[a]	87.6639	81.2677
$r \leq 1$	$r = 2$	48.83	57.6497	53.2201
$r \leq 2$	$r = 3$	20.49	34.4511	31.7246
$r \leq 3$	$r = 4$	7.40	16.2293	14.3547

[a]Denotes significant at 90% confidence level. The 95 and 90% critical values are generated by the bootstrap method using 149 observations and 1000 replications. The underlying VARX trade model is of lag order (4, 3) and contains unrestricted intercept.

Table 1. Cointegrating rank test for VARX (4, 3) trade model.

In order to exactly identify the long-run relationship, we then impose a normalized restriction to produce the long-run estimate of the Malaysia-China trade model (**Table 2**). The log-likelihood ratio (LR) statistic for the normalized (exactly identified) restriction is identical to the value reported in the value of maximized log-likelihood function for the cointegration test. However, the dummy for the subprime mortgage crisis is excluded from the model, as insignificant statistics are reported during the restriction test. Then again, we are aware that for domestic coefficients (*Y*, *PPI*), the asymptotic standard errors are not statistically significant, suggesting that the income and demand effects presence only for foreign (China) variables. It is therefore reasonable to reestimate the cointegration relation by imposing the overidentifying restriction on the variables. Yet, LR tests could over-reject in small samples [24, 33]. The bootstrapped critical values based on 1000 replications of the LR statistic are computed. Using the observed initial values of each variable, the estimated model, and a set of random innovations, an artificial data set is generated for each of the 1000 replications under the assumption that the estimated version of the model is the true data-generating process. The bootstrapped critical values for the joint test are reported at 22.9725 (95% confidence level) and 19.5385 (90% confidence level), while the LR statistic of overidentifying restriction is reported as 22.5245 (p-value = 0.001). Hence, the restriction can be rejected, and the macroeconomic variables included in our trade model are in fact the influential factors. The results also suggest that the presence of the Asian financial crisis (but not the subprime crisis) as a dummy variable does affect the long-run relationships.

$$\ln TB_t = 0.5695\ln Y_t \underset{(1.3174)}{} - 0.4720\ln PPI_t \underset{(0.4131)}{} + 3.0446\ln Q_t \underset{(0.8150)^c}{} - 1.1416\ln Y_t^* \underset{(0.3837)^b}{} + 1.1472\ln PPI_t^* \underset{(0.9775)}{} - 0.3078D97_t \underset{(0.1758)^a}{}$$

95% Bootstrapped CV for LR: 22.9725	LR test: 22.5245 [0.001]
90% Bootstrapped CV for LR: 19.5385	

[a,b,c]Denote significant at the 10, 5, and 1% level, respectively. Asymptotic standard errors are reported in the parentheses ( ) and *p*-value of LR statistics is reported in [ ].

Table 2. Normalized long run estimates and restriction test.

Long-run estimates reported in **Table 2** show that the trade balance is significant and responsive to changes in the real exchange rate of RM/yuan. Recall that the Marshall-Lerner condition implies that a real devaluation of domestic currency (RM) will improve the trade balance only if the sum of the price elasticity of demand for exports and imports is greater that unity. Since the ln*TB* is defined as the ratio of Malaysian exports to imports vis-à-vis China, the reported coefficient of $\ln Q = 3.0446 > 1$ is sufficiently large to support the Marshall-Lerner condition in the long run. As such, we foresee positive trade gains if the Malaysian ringgit is to depreciate against the Chinese yuan, which was evidently true during the Asia financial crisis. Conversely, if devaluation happens for the Chinese yuan, the conflicting feature may emerge because the bilateral imports and exports are sensitive to changes in RM/yuan, which will be reflected in the export and import prices. The finding is a theoretical prediction but not in line with recent studies that failed to support the trade-exchange rate relationship [35, 36].

The modeling of VECMX short-run dynamics is presented in **Table 3** and several points are noteworthy.[6] First of all, the lagged error correction term (ECT_{t-1}) carries its expected negative and significant sign, indicating that the system, once being shocked, will necessarily adjust back to the long-run equilibrium. However, the relatively small coefficient (−0.1933) would imply a rather slow speed of adjustment. Second, the negative lagged $\Delta \ln Q_{t-1}$ followed by a significant and positive lagged $\Delta \ln Q_{t-2}$ seems to support for the J-curve in short run, as suggested by Bahmani-Oskooee and Wang [20]. Third, the dummy for Asia crisis is significant but other lagged endogenous variables are insignificant. As for the exogenous foreign variables, some weak significant lagged effects are detected for Chinese output and producer price.

Despite the R^2 reported as 0.46 in **Table 3**, four additional diagnostic tests are also conducted. For serial correlation, we use the Lagrange multiplier (LM) test. The error correction model is clean of autocorrelation problems as the null hypothesis of serial correlation in residuals failed to be rejected, in the presence of lagged dependent variable. The insignificant *F*-statistic is reported at 1.233 (*p*-value = 0.27) with 12 degrees of freedom. Using the square of the fitted values, the Ramsey Regression Equation Specification Error Test (RESET) then tests for functional misspecification. The model is considered as correctly specified with the *F*-statistic reported as insignificant (*p*-value = 0.67, d.f. = 1). Likewise, the heteroscedasticity test statistic is again insignificant (*p*-value = 0.87). And lastly, the normality tests of skewness and kurtosis

[6]In this chapter, our priority is given to the trade balance model. Hence, only the error correction results for trade balance are presented and discussed. However, estimations for other endogenous variables when taken as independent variables (e.g., *Yt, Qt, Pt*) are available upon request from the corresponding author.

http://dx.doi.org/10.5772/66977

of residuals also do not pose any problem to the VECMX model, with an insignificant chi-squared statistic reported at 3.475 (p-value = 0.18).

	Regressor	Coefficient	Std. error	T-sta (p-value)
Conditional model (endogenous variables)	c	−0.4096[b]	0.1897	-2.1588 (0.033)
	$\Delta \ln TB_{t-1}$	−0.2696[c]	0.0987	-2.7300 (0.007)
	$\Delta \ln TB_{t-2}$	−0.1458[a]	0.0876	−1.6631 (0.099)
	$\Delta \ln TB_{t-3}$	−0.2569[c]	0.0734	-3.4981 (0.001)
	$\Delta \ln Y_{t-1}$	−0.7529[c]	0.2836	-2.6545 (0.009)
	$\Delta \ln Y_{t-2}$	−0.4516	0.3306	−1.3658 (0.174)
	$\Delta \ln Y_{t-3}$	−0.1082	0.2766	−0.39120 (0.696)
	$\Delta \ln PP_{t-1}$	0.5848	0.9505	0.61525 (0.539)
	$\Delta \ln PP_{t-2}$	−0.3194	0.9520	−0.3355 (0.738)
	$\Delta \ln PP_{t-3}$	0.4820	0.9548	0.5048 (0.615)
	$\Delta \ln(Q_{t-1})$	−0.4646	0.4853	−0.9573 (0.340)
	$\Delta \ln(Q_{t-2})$	1.7282[c]	0.4810	3.5932 (0.000)
	$\Delta \ln(Q_{t-3})$	−0.3928	0.5007	−0.7845 (0.434)
	$\Delta D97$	−0.0942[b]	0.0489	−1.9264 (0.044)
	ECT_{t-1}	−0.1933[c]	0.0878	-2.2014 (0.030)
Marginal model (exogenous variables)	$\Delta \ln Y^{*}_{t-1}$	0.8014[a]	0.4192	1.9117 (0.058)
	$\Delta \ln Y^{*}_{t-2}$	0.1541	0.5137	0.30008 (0.765)
	$\Delta \ln Y^{*}_{t-3}$	0.1575	0.4206	0.37436 (0.709)
	$\Delta \ln PP^{*}_{t-1}$	1.5930	1.8617	0.85570 (0.394)
	$\Delta \ln PP^{*}_{t-2}$	4.5957[b]	2.1936	2.0950 (0.038)
	$\Delta \ln PP^{*}_{t-3}$	-3.0073	1.9446	−1.5465 (0.124)
Diagnostic tests				
R^2	AUTO	RESET	Normal	Hetero
0.46	1.233 (0.27)	0.183 (0.67)	3.475 (0.18)	0.026 (0.87)

[a, b, c] Denote significant at the 10, 5, and 1% level, respectively. AUTO is the LM test for serial correlation; RESET is the Ramsey Reset test for functional form; Normal is a test that examine for normality in the errors; and Hetero tests for heteroscedasticity. Except the Normal test that uses chi-squared statistics, all diagnostic tests are conducted using the F-statistics.

Table 3. Error correction representation of the VECMX trade model.

A subsequent and important inspection of model stability is to apply the cumulative sum (CUSUM) and cumulative sum of squares (CUSUMSQ) tests to the residuals of the error-correction VECMX model and the long-run VARX coefficient estimates. For the CUSUM test, the recursive residuals are plotted against the break points, while the CUSUMSQ plots the squared recursive residuals against the break points. As a graphical presentation, these two statistics are then plotted within two straight lines, which are bounded by 5% significance level. If any point lay beyond this 5% level, the null hypothesis of stable parameters is rejected or otherwise. Clearly, **Figure 1** shows that the stability of estimated coefficients for our Malaysia-China trade model as both statistics is within the critical lines.

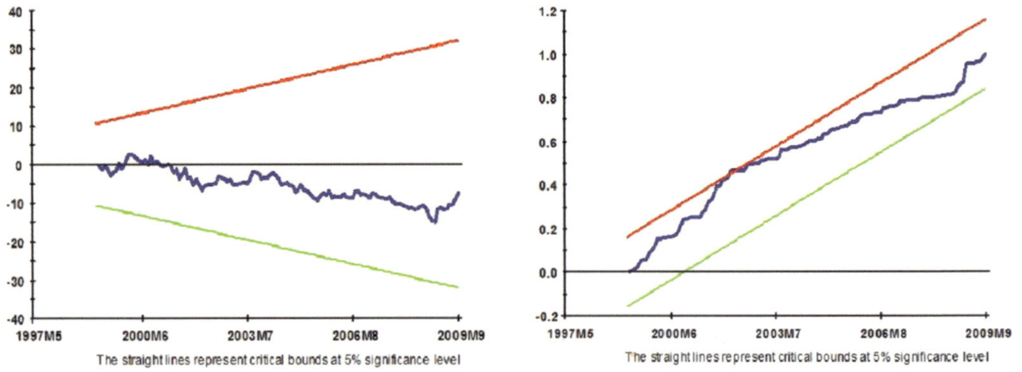

Figure 1. Diagnostic tests of CUSUM and CUSUMSQ.

3.2. Shock responses and speed of convergence

A good way of measuring the speed of convergence of the cointegrating relations to equilibrium is to examine the dynamic responses of the endogenous variables to various types of shocks, in particular shocks to the real RM/yuan, Malaysian output, and prices. We first consider the effect of system-wide shocks on the cointegrating relations using the persistence profile developed by Pesaran and Shin [37]. On impact, the persistence profile is normalized to take the value of unity, but the rate at which it tends toward zero provides information on the speed with which the equilibrium correction takes place in response to shocks. In addition to the point estimates, the 95% confidence bounds—which are generated by employing the nonparametric bootstrap method using 1000 replications—are also illustrated as dotted lines (**Figure 2**). The system-wide shock has affected all long-run relations significantly in the beginning, before the effects eventually disappear in the long run. The half-life is about 2 months, and the whole effect takes around 6 months to complete. The result seems to be consistent with the error correction process of the VECMX model.

Next, to analyze the effect of a shock to a variable on the expected future values of the endogenous variables, we employ the generalized IRFs, which measure the change to the n-period forecast of each of the variables that would be caused by a shock to the particular variable. In contrast to the orthogonalized impulse response, the generalized IRFs do not require orthogonalization of shocks and are invariant to the ordering of the variables in the VAR [38] and in our case, the VARX model. In this section, we first consider the responses of the trade balance variable to a positive unit shock of most concerned endogenous variable, the real RM/yuan.

As shown in **Figure 3**, a unit shock (depreciation) of the real RM/yuan is followed by the response of an expansion in trade balance series. The impact lasted about a year and stabilized in the 13th

http://dx.doi.org/10.5772/66977

month. When there is currency devaluation, we generally expect that the trade balance deteriorates at first, because the price change occurs quickly, while trade quantities (volume) change more slowly. After a moderate time period, the volume effect becomes large enough to offset the price effect and the trade balance improves to exhibit the so-called J-curve phenomenon. However, in **Figure 3**, a 1% depreciation of the Malaysian ringgit brings about a 6% gain in the trade balance almost immediately—in the first 2.5 months—which lowers to a 3% gain in the following months. In other words, depreciation of the RM/yuan resulted in an overall trade surplus for Malaysia against China, where the price effect failed to dominate the volume effect even in the early stage. Perhaps, this is the result of Chinese imports growing faster than exports (against ASEAN) in recent years. Though there is no clear pattern of a J-curve for Malaysia-China bilateral trade, the finding is consistent with the long-run estimation that the bilateral trade is sensitive to real exchange rate changes.

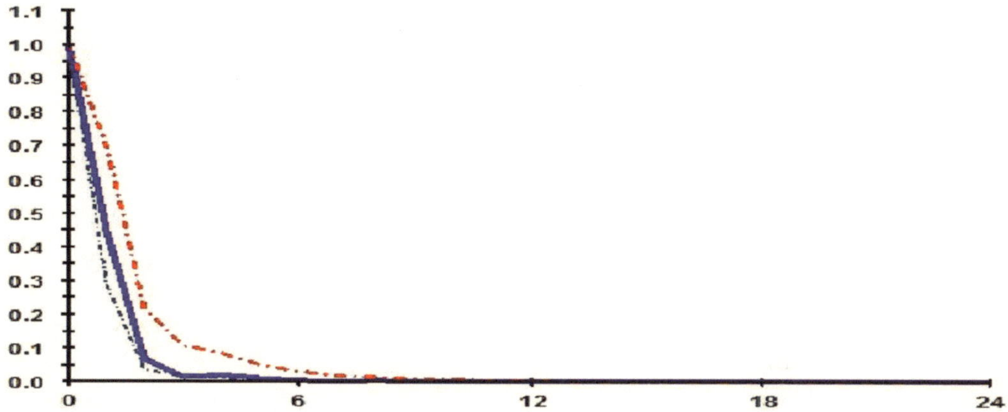

Figure 2. Persistence profile of a system-wide shock to cointegrating relation.

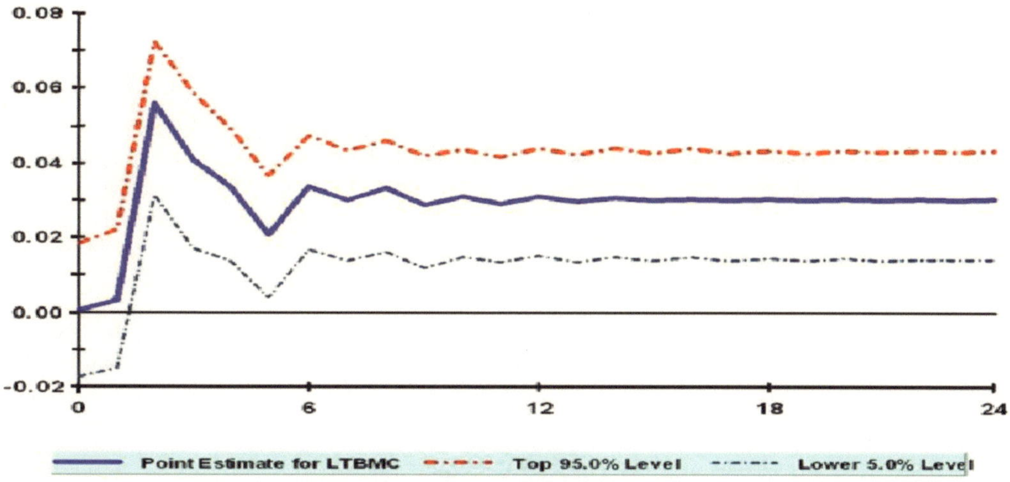

Figure 3. Response of Malaysia-China trade balance to real RM/yuan shock.

The generalized IRFs of the trade balance to a unit shock in output and producer prices are given in **Figure 4**. The result indicates the extent to which demand and supply channels affect the bilateral trade balances. The trade balance series depicts a V-shape adjustment to Malaysian output (industrial production) shocks. Domestic consumers may increase their demand for Chinese goods due to the income effect, resulting in temporal trade balance deterioration, but this effect gradually ends within a year. Response to foreign (China) output demonstrates a similar magnitude effect, though the impact lasts longer, about 15 months. This could be due to the substitution effect under which Chinese consumers shift their demand for Malaysian exports to other goods and services. Conversely, IRFs of trade balance responses to Malaysian and Chinese producer prices follow an increasing path. The impacts remain positive and stabilize within a year. The figure seems to indicate some early signs of trade expansion following the producer price shocks.

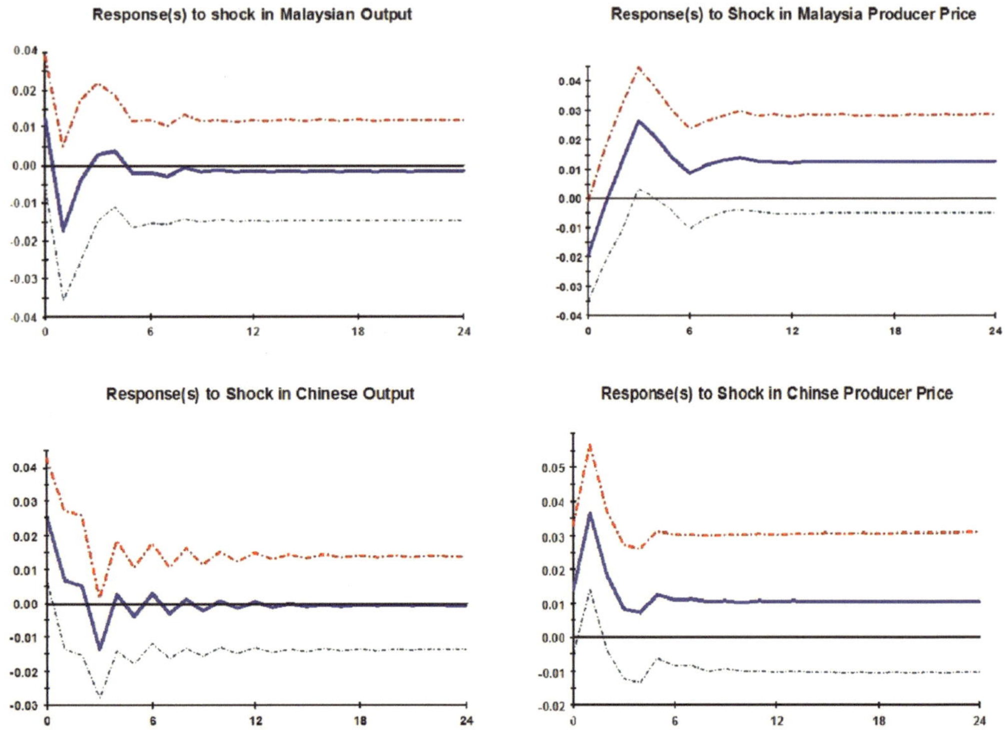

Figure 4. Responses of Malaysia-China trade balance to shocks in output and prices.

The effects of real exchange rate shock on output and producer prices are shown in **Figure 5**. The point estimates are bounded by the 95% bootstrapped confidence intervals using 1000 replications. Clearly, Malaysia shows a greater response to the foreign exchange rate shock, perhaps due to the greater openness of the Malaysian economy. However, a positive unit shock (depreciation) of real RM/yuan is contractionary for Malaysian output. An initial 1%

depreciation of the Malaysian ringgit results in a 1.2% reduction in industrial production in the first 2 months. The impact stabilizes after 8 months at approximately 0.8% below its base value. Such a finding of the contractionary effect due to devaluation is along the lines of studies by Rajan and Shen [39], Ahmed et al. [40], and Bahmani-Oskooee and Miteza [36]. Indeed, Kim and Ying [41] have underlined that devaluation may be more contractionary than previously thought because of financial liberalization and improvement in information technology; devaluation worsens the balance of payments of countries with heavy foreign currency liabilities. There is also an adverse effect on the country's reputation, impairing its ability to raise foreign capital.

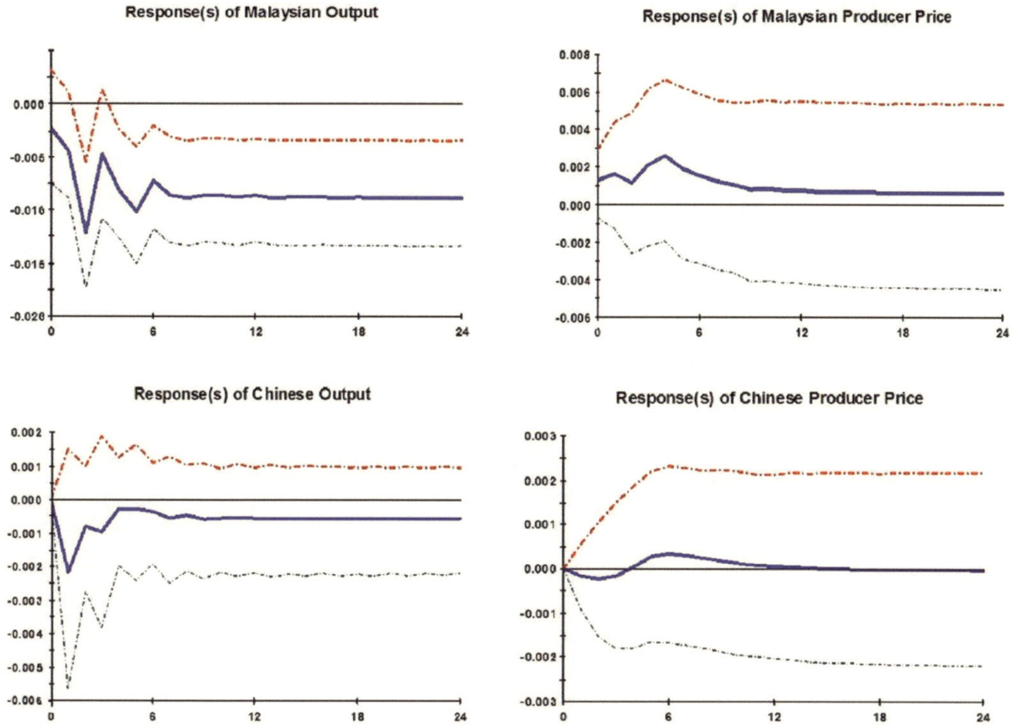

Figure 5. Response(s) of output and prices to positive unit shocks in real RM/yuan.

Likewise, Chinese output responds negatively to the positive shock of RM/yuan (in which the yuan appreciates), but the impact is minor. The deterioration of production (about 0.2%) is observed in the second and third months and the impact stabilizes after 9 months at approximately 0.1% below its base value. Keep in mind that China practices an export-led growth policy based on maintenance of an undervalued yuan. The finding may partly justify China's rigid policy of keeping the yuan from appreciating against world currencies in the past decade. On the other hand, the response(s) of producer prices to foreign exchange shocks are muted and are generally insignificant statistically. As for the Malaysian producer price shock, the impact could be slightly inflationary, but the scale is small. It is still inconclusive whether devaluation has inflationary or deflationary effects.

Subsequent analysis uses the variance decompositions (VDCs) in an attempt to gauge the extent of shocks to a variable that can be explained by other variables considered in the VARX model. **Table 4** presents the generalized VDCs for our VARX model. VDCs can be considered as an out-sample causality test, which provides a quantitative measurement of how much the movement in one variable can be explained by other variables in the VAR system in terms of the percentage of forecast error variance. However, the results based on conventional orthogonalized VDCs are found to be sensitive to the number of lag lengths used and the ordering of the variables in the equation. The errors in any equation in a VAR are normally serially uncorrelated by construction, but there may be contemporaneous correlations across errors of different equations. To overcome this problem, the generalized VDCs of forecast error are applied [42].

	Horizon	**% of variance explained by innovations in**					
		TB	**Y**	**PP**	**Q**	**Y***	**PP***
TB	4	**70.78**	1.29	4.48	15.76	2.39	5.22
	8	**68.77**	0.95	4.28	17.95	1.77	4.69
	12	**67.56**	0.75	4.30	19.25	1.39	4.29
	16	**66.80**	0.63	4.29	20.12	1.14	4.04
	20	**66.29**	0.54	4.27	20.71	0.96	3.86
	24	**65.92**	0.47	4.26	21.14	0.84	3.72
Y	4	5.51	**65.68**	2.03	6.50	8.80	20.28
	8	7.47	**53.76**	1.73	7.94	10.63	28.94
	12	8.64	**48.46**	1.69	8.35	11.30	32.75
	16	9.39	**45.43**	1.68	8.63	11.66	34.77
	20	9.89	**43.53**	1.69	8.80	11.89	36.01
	24	10.23	**42.23**	1.69	8.92	12.04	36.85
PP	4	1.82	2.22	**89.14**	1.04	0.19	8.87
	8	0.93	1.35	**85.38**	0.75	0.13	10.65
	12	0.83	1.00	**83.04**	0.53	0.08	11.43
	16	0.83	0.82	**81.72**	0.41	0.06	11.81
	20	0.85	0.71	**80.92**	0.34	0.05	12.03
	24	0.86	0.64	**80.38**	0.29	0.04	12.17
Q	4	6.68	0.47	5.79	**78.70**	5.23	6.16
	8	22.15	1.38	4.52	**61.91**	3.80	6.50
	12	29.73	1.83	4.23	**53.26**	3.10	6.48

	Horizon	% of variance explained by innovations in					
		TB	Y	PP	Q	Y*	PP*
	16	34.11	2.10	4.08	**48.27**	2.70	6.41
	20	36.91	2.27	3.99	**45.09**	2.44	6.36
	24	38.82	2.39	3.92	**42.90**	2.27	6.32
Y*	4	0.13	0.04	1.97	0.27	**97.37**	2.38
	8	0.17	0.04	2.33	0.19	**97.07**	2.03
	12	0.17	0.03	2.41	0.16	**96.99**	1.86
	16	0.16	0.03	2.46	0.14	**96.95**	1.76
	20	0.16	0.02	2.50	0.13	**96.92**	1.70
	24	0.16	0.02	2.52	0.13	**96.89**	1.65
PP*	4	0.27	0.13	8.81	0.01	3.31	**90.90**
	8	0.21	0.11	11.78	0.02	2.82	**87.87**
	12	0.13	0.08	12.79	0.02	2.71	**86.67**
	16	0.10	0.07	13.26	0.01	2.67	**86.04**
	20	0.07	0.06	13.53	0.01	2.66	**85.66**
	24	0.06	0.05	13.70	0.01	2.65	**85.42**

Note: Bold values are referring to the % of variance explained by own innovations.

Table 4. Generalized variance decomposition.

In **Table 4**, the Chinese variables (industrial production and producer price) seem to be the most exogenous variables among the six variables in the system. Most of the shocks are explained by their own innovations (87–97%) over the horizon of 24 months. Such a finding provides the methodological support for the VARX and VECMX modeling approach employed in this study. On the other hand, trade balance and real foreign exchange rates are found to be endogenous. In line with the long-run estimates, innovation from the real foreign exchange rate explains a substantial portion of the forecast error variance in the trade balance (about 20%). As for the foreign exchange rate, the major innovation comes from Chinese producer price. Yet, the Malaysian producer price is relatively exogenously determined, though it was included in the conditional model as an endogenous variable.

4. Conclusion and policy implications

The present study explores the dynamic relationship of trade balance, exchange rates, outputs (demand), and producer prices (supply) for Malaysia-China in the era of global crises, e.g. Asia financial crisis, subprime crisis. The empirical framework was constructed based on the VARX and VECMX modeling procedures. In addition, the application of persistent profile and IRFs shows how the core variables (*TB, Y, PP, Q*) evolve with respect to economic shocks.

With additional scrutiny of generalized VDCs and forecasting assessment, the comprehensive analyses allow us to draw useful insights about the Marshall-Lerner condition, the J-curve phenomenon, and the output (expansion or contraction) and price effects (inflationary or deflationary) between Malaysia and China.

First of all, the Marshall-Lerner condition holds for Malaysia against China in the long run. The short-run J-curve pattern is not visible through the IRF analysis but noticeable in the error correction modeling. This would suggest a potential gain in Malaysian balance of payment if ringgit depreciated against the yuan. Theoretically, in a Keynesian economy with excess capacity, devaluation boosts net exports and, through the multiplier effect, fosters economic growth. Such demand channel, however, does not work well in the Malaysia-China case during and after the Asia financial crisis. Based on the generalized IRFs, a positive unit shock of real RM/yuan (in which RM depreciates) results in a contractionary effect for Malaysian output. If we refer to the generalized VDC analysis, the percentage variance of industrial production is not well explained by the innovations in variance of the real foreign exchange. Moreover, domestic and foreign incomes are only significant through lagged effects in the short-run model but not in the long-run model, suggesting that the demand side effects are temporal. In other words, devaluation for export gains is insufficient to sustain output expansion for Malaysia against China. It is worth noting that the success of currency depreciation in improving the trade balance largely depends on switching demand in the suitable direction and amount, as well as on the capacity of the home economy to fulfill the additional demand by supplying more goods. Since the trade expansion due to currency shock is temporal and the short-run adjustments are slow, productivity growth in real and tradable sectors is essentially vital to enhance the external competitiveness and hence economic growth.

From the supply side's viewpoint, Malaysia is a typical semi-industrialized nation, where inputs for manufacturing are still largely imported and not produced domestically due to deficiency in economy of scale; for instance, the automobile, the chemical and allied industry production and textile manufacturing. Firms' input cost may increase following currency devaluation. However, our analysis of IRFs has not shown clear inflationary or deflationary effect following the shock in real Malaysian ringgit. And, the lagged variables of the producer price were statistically insignificant in the error correction modeling of VECMX. Both the Malaysian and Chinese producer prices are also relatively exogenously determined, as indicated by the VDC analysis. At the outset, the results suggest that negative impact from the higher cost of imported inputs from China (due to ringgit depreciation) does not dominate the production stimulus from lower relative prices for domestically traded goods. In other words, China has yet to be Malaysia's main source of imported inflation.

At the present stage, China has shown complementary features and been supportive of regional trading. In mid-August 2010, China began the trading of Malaysian ringgit against the yuan on its domestic foreign exchange market to promote bilateral trade between the two nations and to facilitate the use of the yuan to settle cross-border trade. Yet, the potential conflicting (competing) aspect of the trade relationship cannot be ignored. Manufacturing accounted for 92.4% of China's merchandise exports in 2006, and the trend persists. Malaysia remains competitive in machinery, electronic equipment, and energy supply, but not competitive in clothing and textile manufacturing, food, agricultural and leather-related products, and transportation. Malaysia needs to upgrade its export structure and reduce low-end and labor-intensive manufacturing. Malaysia's focus should be on high value-added production, design, and service sectors, before China overtakes it in these areas. Since both nations are now promoting the respective services sectors, further bilateral liberalization and strategic collaboration in services trading should be an important focus of Malaysia-China trade. These services may include education, medical tourism, transportation, and construction, as well as financial services. The two nations could experience economic gains in market structure and product diversification as well as economies of scale from regional trade integration. In addition, both nations have committed to bilateral trade integration, in addition to support for the multilateral framework within the ASEAN+6 regimes. Despite the strong competition in manufacturing exports, China recognizes Malaysia as an influential player within ASEAN and various ASEAN-driven collaboration platforms, such as the ASEAN Regional Forum and the East Asian Summit. The trade expansion is likely to accelerate with the formalization of a bilateral trade liberalization pact on track under the ASEAN-China Free Trade Agreement.

Acknowledgements

This research was supported by a research university grant from Universiti Sains Malaysia (grant no: 1001/PPAMC/816241). The usual disclaimer applies.

Author details

Tze-Haw Chan

Address all correspondence to: thchan@usm.my

Graduate School of Business (GSB), Universiti Sains Malaysia (USM), Penang, Malaysia

References

[1] Cheong, Y. R., "The Impact of China's Entrance to the WTO on Neighboring East Asian Economies," *China Economic Review*, vol. 11, no. 4, pp. 419–422, 2001.

[2] Hai, W., "China's WTO Membership: Significance and Implications," China Center for Economic Research (CCER), Working Paper No. E2000007, 2000.

[3] Wang, V. W.-C., "The Logic of China-ASEAN FTA: Economic Statecraft of "Peaceful Ascendancy," in *Southeast Asia and China: Global Changes and Regional Challenges,* Ho, K.-L. and Ku, S. (eds.). Singapore: Institute of Southeast Asia Studies, 2005, pp. 17–41..

[4] Chan, T. H. and C. W. Hooy, "Role of Exchange Rate on China-Malaysia Long Run Trading: Complementary or Conflicting?," *Malaysian Journal of Economic Studies*, vol. 49, no. 2, pp. 157–177, 2012.

[5] Lall, S., "Reinventing Industrial Strategy: The Role of Government Policy in Building Industrial Competitiveness," in *United Nations Conference on Trade and Development*, 2004, pp. G-24 Discussion Papers 28.

[6] Chan, T. H., A. Z. Baharumshah and R. Khong, "Dynamic Financial Linkages of Japan and ASEAN Economies: An Application of Real Interest Parity," *Capital Markets Review, Special Issue*, vol. 11, no. 1 & 2, pp. 23–40, 2003.

[7] Chan, T. H. and A. Z. Baharumshah, "Chapter 5: Financial Integration between China and Asia Pacific," in *Emerging Markets and Financial Resilience: Decoupling Growth from Turbulence,* Hooy, C. W., Ali, R. and Ghon Rhee, S. (eds.). Palgrave McMillan, 2013, pp. 63–84.

[8] Lall, S. and M. Albaladejo, "China's Competitive Performance: A Threat to East Asian Manufactured Exports?," *World Development*, vol. 32, pp. 1441–1466, 2004.

[9] Zhang, Y. and G.-H. Wan, "What Accounts for China's Trade Balance Dynamics?," *Journal of Policy Modeling*, vol. 29, no. 6, pp. 821–883, 2007.

[10] Greenaway, D., A. Mahabir and C. Milner, "Has China Displaced Other Asian Countries' Exports?," *China Economic Review*, vol. 19, no. 2, pp. 152–169, 2008.

[11] Makin, J., *Two New Paradigms*. Washington, DC: American Enterprise Institute, 1997.

[12] Corsetti, G., P. Pesenti and N. Roubini, "What Caused the Asian Currency and Financial Crisis?," *Japan and the World Economy*, vol. 11, no. 3, pp. 305–373, 1999.

[13] Arroba, A. A., R. Avendaño, and J. Estrada, World Economic Forum, OECD Development Centre, 2007 [Online]. http://www.weforum.org/pdf/Latin_America/OECD.pdf

[14] Chen, I. T.-Y. and A. H. Yang, "A Harmonized Southeast Asia? Explanatory Typologies of ASEAN Countries' Strategies to the Rise of China," *The Pacific Review*, vol. 26, no. 3, pp. 265–288, 2013.

[15] Chan, T. H., H. H. Lean and C. W. Hooy, "A Macro Assessment of China Effects on Malaysian Exports and Trade Balances," *Journal of Chinese Economic and Foreign Trade Studies*, vol. 7, no. 1, pp. 18–37, 2014.

[16] Baharumshah, A. Z., "The Effect of Exchange Rate on Bilateral Trade Balance: New Evidence from Malaysia and Thailand," *Asian Economic Journal*, vol. 3, pp. 291–312, 2001.

[17] Ahmad, J. and J. Yang, "Estimation of the J-Curve in China. East-West Center," Working Papers No. 67, 2004.

[18] Bahmani-Oskooee, M. and H. Harvey, "How Sensitive Are Malaysia's Bilateral Trade Flows to Depreciation?," *Applied Economics*, vol. 38, pp. 1279–1286, 2006.

[19] Bahmani-Oskooee, M. and H. Harvey, "The J-Curve: Malaysia versus Her Major Trading Partners," *Applied Economics*, vol. 42, pp. 1067–1076, 2010.

[20] Bahmani-Oskooee, M. and Y. Wang, "The J Curve: China versus Her Trading Partners," *Bulletin of Economic Research*, vol. 4, pp. 323–343, 2006.

[21] Yong Jian, E., A. Y. Gu and C.-C. Yang, "Real Exchange Rate Behavior under Peg: Evidence from the Chinese RMB and Malaysian MYR," *Review of Pacific Basin Financial Markets and Policies*, vol. 12, no. 1, pp. 141–158, 2009.

[22] Pesaran, M. H., Y. Shin and R. J. Smith, "Structural Analysis of Vector Error Correction Models with Exogenous *I*(1) Variables," *Journal of Econometrics*, vol. 97, pp. 293–343, 2000.

[23] Garratt, A., K. Lee, M. H. Pesaran and Y. Shin, "A Long Run Structural Macro-Econometric Model of the UK," *Economic Journal*, vol. 113, pp. 412–455, 2003.

[24] Garratt, A., K. Lee, M. H. Pesaran and Y. Shin, *Global and National Macroeconometric Modeling: A Long Run Structural Approach*. Oxford: Oxford University Press, 2008.

[25] Assenmacher-Wesche, K. and M. H. Pesaran, "A VECX* Model of the Swiss Economy," Swiss National Bank (SNB) Economic Studies Working Paper 2009–6, 2009.

[26] Smith, L. V. and A. Galesi, GVAR Toolbox 1.1, 2011 [Online]. www.cfap.jbs.cam.ac.uk/research/gvartoolbox (accessed 16 July 2012).

[27] Saikkonen, P. and H. Lütkepohl, "Testing for a Unit Root in a Time Series with a Level Shift at Unknown Time," *Econometric Theory*, vol. 18, pp. 313–348, 2002.

[28] Mantalos, P. and G. Shukur, "Size and Power of the Error Correction Model Cointegration Test. A Bootstrap Approach," *Oxford Bulletin of Economics and Statistics*, vol. 60, pp. 249–255, 1998.

[29] Chang, Y., J. Y. Park and K. Song, "Bootstrapping Cointegrating Regressions," *Journal of Econometrics*, vol. 133, pp. 703–739, 2006.

[30] Shirvani, H. and B. Wilbratte, "The Relationship between the Real Exchange Rate and the Trade Balance: An Empirical Reassessment," *International Economic Journal*, vol. 11, no. 1, pp. 39–50, 1997.

[31] Kandil, M. and A. Mirzaie, "The Effects of Exchange Rate Fluctuations on Output and Prices: Evidence from Developing Countries," *Journal of Developing Areas*, vol. 38, pp. 189–219, 2005.

[32] Lumsdaine, R. L. and D. H. Papell, "Multiple Trend Breaks and the Unit-Root Hypothesis," *Review of Economics and Statistics*, vol. 9, no. 2, pp. 212–218, 1997.

[33] Affandi, Y., "A Small Monetary System for Indonesia: A Long Run Structural Approach," unpublished Ph.D. thesis, Cambridge, 2007.

[34] Johansen, S. and K. Juselius, "Maximum Likelihood Estimation and Inference on Cointegration—with Applications to the Demand for Money," *Oxford Bulletin of Economics and Statistics*, vol. 52, no. 2, pp. 169–210, 1990.

[35] Rose, A. K. and J. L. Yellen, "Is There a J-Curve?," *Journal of Monetary Economics*, vol. 24, no. 1, pp. 53–68, 1989.

[36] Bahmani-Oskooee, M. and I. Miteza, "Are Devaluations Expansionary or Contractionary? A Survey Article," *Economic Issues*, vol. 2, pp. 1–28, 2003.

[37] Pesaran, M. H. and Y. Shin, "Cointegration and Speed of Convergence to Equilibrium," *Journal of Econometrics*, vol. 71, pp. 117–143, 1996.

[38] Pesaran, M. H. and Y. Shin, "Generalised Impulse Response Analysis in Linear Multivariate Models," *Economics Letters*, vol. 1, pp. 17–29, 1998.

[39] Rajan, R. S. and C.-H. Shen, "Are Crisis-Induced Devaluations Contractionary?," Federal Reserve Bank of San Francisco, Pacific Basin Working Paper Series 02–06 2002.

[40] Ahmed, S., C. J. Gust, S. B. Kamin and J. Huntley, "Are Depreciations as Contractionary as Devaluations? A Comparison of Selected Emerging and Industrial Economies," Board of Governors of the Federal Reserve System, Washington, D.C., International Finance Discussion Paper No. 737, 2002.

[41] Kim, Y. and Y. H. Ying, "An Empirical Assessment of Currency Devaluation in East Asian Countries," *Journal of International Money and Finance*, vol. 26, no. 2, pp. 265–283, 2007.

[42] Pesaran, M. H. and B. Pesaran, *Working with Microfit 4.0: Interactive Econometric Analysis* [Windows Version]. Oxford: Oxford University Press, 1997.

Chapter 6

Tourism Invisible Part of Exports: The Analysis of Slovenia and Montenegro on the Chinese Outbound Tourism

Andrej Raspor, Ana Stranjančević, Iva Bulatović and Darko Lacmanović

Additional information is available at the end of the chapter

http://dx.doi.org/10.5772/66628

Abstract

People's Republic of China is the largest, Slovenia is the 64th and Montenegro is the 162nd largest export economy in the world. Methods of analysis, deduction and induction and comparative method were used in this paper. The paper reviews and analyzes statistical data of international trade with China as well as of Chinese outbound tourism and provides an estimate of what share Slovenia and Montenegro received. Starting off with the research question 'Are the revenue from the export of China and revenue from Chinese inbound tourism ('invisible export') in gross domestic product (GDP) growing?' we have concluded that China is becoming a more important partner for both countries. There is a strong positive correlation between exports in China and the number of overnights of Chinese tourists both in Slovenia and Montenegro and that expenditure of Chinese tourists visiting these two countries increases every year as well. Expenditure and share of expenditure of Chinese tourists visiting Slovenia and Montenegro in Chinese exports increase every year. Share of expenditure of Chinese tourists and export in Chinese GDP increase every year.

Keywords: Chinese tourists, Chinese outbound tourism, exports, consumption, Montenegro, Slovenia

1. Introduction

The aim of this paper is to analyze the relationship between international trade and tourism regarding economic growth in Slovenia and Montenegro.

The interest for the topic arises because the existing literature pays small attention to economic effects (through international trade) by international tourism in area of Western Balkan countries such as Slovenia and Montenegro when it comes from Chinese outbound tourism. This paper highlights the importance of Chinese outbound tourism flow and main influence to international trade as source of economic growth in stated countries.

The main research question was dedicated to determining whether the revenue from the export in China and from the Chinese inbound tourism ('invisible export') in GDP is growing or not.

The paper is organized through three parts and introduction. Part one deals with the literature review of international trade and tourism in context of economic growth. Part two presents empirical evidence of the main effects of Chinese inbound tourism as an 'invisible export' of China in Slovenia and Montenegro. Part three discusses the main empirical findings in literature context, offers some conclusions and explains limitations of this paper and direction of future research.

2. International trade and tourism in context of economic growth

Economic valourization of tourism is expressed through tourist spending. The scope and structure of tourism consumption are the result of qualitative and quantitative composition of the tourism product in destination and any microeconomic tourism entity, respectively [1]. Determining the scope, structure and effects of tourist spending at the level of international, national, regional or local economy represents a methodological problem due to the complexity of tourism as a socio-economic phenomenon [2]. Tourism in terms of economic activity is treated as an 'invisible export' [3] due to the fact that consumption of goods and services by foreign tourists really carries out the export on the spot in a tourist destination.

The relationship of tourism and international trade is defined based on the impact of foreign tourist spending at both national and international level. According to UNWTO data, tourism revenues account for about 30% of world exports of services, 6% of the total world exports and about 9% of world GDP [4]. The continuous growth of the global tourism market is encouraging, given that the rate of growth of international tourism arrivals, from 1980 to the present, between 3.9 and 4.4% and in the future up to 2030 is projected rate to 3.3% [4]. On the other hand, trade representing 20 to 40% of the budget of the average consumer of the tourist during the trip [5], which largely depends on the level of development of tourist destinations including the trade activity, or in other words it can be said that the development of trade in the tourism market is in correlation with the level of foreign exchange effect.

UNWTO predicted economic output growth caused by tourism flows for the period 2010–2030 in all regions: Asia (+5.7% a year), Africa (+4.8%), Middle East (+4.3%), Americas and Europe (+2.6%) and worldwide (+4.0%) [6].

Mutual influence of international trade and tourism is the subject of continuous attention to a large number of studies in the field of economics of tourism, as follows.

Using relation between tourism and trade, it could be stated that 'in terms of international trade, tourism is part of trade in services. For a national economy receipts from international

http://dx.doi.org/10.5772/66628

tourism count as exports, while expenditure on international tourism outside the national economy counts as imports' [7], also international tourism could be defined as 'a form of trade that represents exports as tourist arrivals' [8].

In theoretical context regarding relationship among tourism, trade and economic growth, there is 'the tourism-led growth (TLG) hypothesis, which postulates the existence of a positive relationship between the earnings from international tourism and economic growth, remains the fundamental justification for tourism's inclusion in regional and development strategies' [9], or in other words 'the relationship between international trade and international travel is tautological since international travel forms part of the international service sector transactions of a country's balance of payments' [10].

Measuring the impact of tourism on GDP, there were two widely accepted methodologies such as tourism satellite account (TSA) and computable general equilibrium (CGE) models [11].

By the TSA the size and impact of tourism on the economic activities explicitly included in the system of national accounts (SNA) through different variables such as gross value added (GVA) in tourism characteristic activities are measured.

In CGE models over input-output models, it focuses on the impact on GDP through, for example, increasing in foreign tourism expenditure (removal indirect taxes) and air transport productivity. This model 'simulates what will happen in the economy as a consequence of external shocks but does not state what has already happened' [11].

Summarizing the results of the United Nations Conference on Trade and Development Expert Meeting on Strengthening the Capacity for Expanding the Tourism Sector in Developing Countries, held in 1998, regarding the tourism economic impact, it could be pointed out [12]:

- The international tourism industry had the highest multiplier and positive spillover effects regarding all other economic sectors.
- Tourism could stimulate development in terms of income, employment, foreign-exchange earnings, taxation and multiplier and spillover effects.
- In international trade in tourism services in developing countries consistently had surpluses.
- International tourism receipts provided foreign-exchange earnings and stabilized countries' total foreign currency receipts and provided a cushion against the instability of merchandize exports with some 'leakages' due to increased import activities.

By researching the features and determinants of the international travel and tourism service trade between 37 countries from European, Asian and North American regions during period 2000–2005, additional facts [13] were revealed.

From the global perspective, economic size has significant positive effects in promoting international travel and tourism exports, but without apparent home market effect in terms of international service trade theory, which is very close to the well-known theoretical attitude about the effect on GDP concerning international and domestic tourism flows [14].

Travel service exports in home countries are inelastic to the appreciation of domestic currencies, meaning that policy of depreciation of currency is not desirable in promoting travel and tourism trade export which is rather in contrary to theoretical assumptions about currency policy in tourism.

The growth of the trade in goods influences mainly international business travel as 'spillover effect from goods trade has significantly positive signs for all pairs of regions apart from the Europe-North America and North America-Europe pairs of regions' [13].

Investigated the impact of tourism on economic growth, by employing with data for 174 countries in period 2000–2010 [15], the strongest contribution in Africa, Asia, Latin America and Caribbean (Macao SAR, Maldives and Cape Verde on country level) was observed, while in Europe, North America and Oceania, negative impact was noticed slightly. Stronger contribution was noticed in countries where tourism accounts for a higher share of gross domestic product (GDP). It is also observed that tourism did not contribute in least developed countries (LDCs) more than other countries and in conclusion remarks are stated that 'neither the size of the population or economy of a country, nor the wealth or the amount of travel and tourism GDP of a country have any significant influence on tourism's actual contribution to economic growth' [15] which is in contrary to previous research results [13] and implies more complex approach to determine real tourism's impact according to tourism-led growth (TLG) hypothesis [9, 16].

In a study which deals with the relationship between tourism and economic growth in a dynamic model of international trade [17], it was pointed 'endogenous growth model in which tourism is the growth engine of the economy and balanced growth is assured thanks to the quality of tourist services being kept constant' [17], and in that case, 'tourism allows the imports of foreign capital to be financed' [17].

In research regarding relationship between tourism exports, imports of capital goods and economic growth [18], it was stressed 'a mechanism of international transmission of growth from the foreign country (the tourism services importer) to the domestic economy (the tourism services exporter) through trade and terms-of-trade movements without any technological progress, R&D activity or accumulation of human capital in the latter' [18], which suggests more tourism product differentiation in order to make faster economic growth. Research results also made clear 'the two channels of the impact of tourism exports on growth (improvement of the efficiency of productive resources (…) and increase in the quantity of productive resources' [18].

Kulendran and Wilson in their research [10] proved the idea that long-run relationship between international trade and international travel exists, but a strong link when it comes to imports was not found.

Fayed and Fletcher stressed international tourism as major force in globalization of international trade, source of income and employment and important factor in the balance of payments. In that sense, authors notice that tourism is the main sector in international trade in service in many developing countries [19], which is one of the possibilities for balanced economic and sustainable development worldwide.

http://dx.doi.org/10.5772/66628

Examining the international tourism specialization of small countries, it could be noted that tourism is an important factor of economic growth in the case that is elasticity of substitution between manufacturing goods and tourism services less than 1 [20], with important findings that 'an increase in world GDP of only 1% leads to a rise in tourism revenues of about 5,8%' [20].

Analyzing the economic structure of world tourism, Vu and Turner [8] indicate that the main world regional international tourism flows from developed to less developed countries and create a process of foreign-exchange income in same direction but without strong evidence that the main flow of receipt was to the developing world. However, authors noticed the 'unique role' of tourism 'not only in terms of the transfer of wealth from the developed to the developing world, but also in terms of shifting the emphasis of wealth creation, in the developing world, from agrarian, mining and cheap labour manufactures to service industry employment [8].

By applying a panel econometric approach on the standard tourism demand, Gunter and Smeral, stated that income elasticities through different growth periods of total tourism exports showed significant variations and tend to decline. The highest income elasticities observed in period 1977–1992 and the lowest one (lower than 1) in period 2004–2013 due to 'dramatic deterioration in the economic environment contributing to higher uncertainty about the future (…) liquidity constraints limited expenditures on luxuries, (…) preferred domestic destinations instead of going abroad' as authors noted [21], and that is a very interesting fact in context of mutual influence among international tourism industry and trade. This raises the question about long-term tourism flows and expected receipts in tourism destinations in spite of optimistic UNWTO forecasts [6].

Keum pointed in his research about relationship between international tourism and trade on the fact that 'a successful policy causing more international tourism interchanges with specific countries can be an essential condition for successful bilateral free trade agreements (FTA) (…) that the exchanges in tourism, such as people and culture, were accompanied by the exchanges of goods' [22] which means that promotion of tourism flows strongly encouraged the development of international trade.

Investigating long-run, short-run and contemporaneous relationship across international per capita tourism arrivals, real GDP and share of total commercial transaction on GDP for the Italian economy, by using structural vector error correction model (SVECM) [23], it was found that real GDP 'while causing trade, is characterized by a reciprocal, reinforcing mechanism from tourism expansion' [23]. Another observation, in same research, concerns a very fast reaction by tourism and trade regarding to real GDP shocks and much longer time for GDP stabilization after tourism and trade shocks.

In a very recent research about causality between tourism and trade, Hong et al. report about 'long-run equilibrium relationship between business travel and the bilateral trade volumes between Hong Kong and US' [24] concluding that 'increase in business visitation (…) will positively affect (…) economic development' [24], and in that case, it is important to notice that results of this study are 'largely consistent with prior literature regarding the causality relationship between business travel and trade or economic development in a country' [24].

Discussing the tourism and empirical applications of international trade theory by a multi-country analysis, Webster et al. [25] found that many countries specialize in inbound and outbound tourism flows which had common basics with international trade theory as authors noted in 'international differences in technology and factor endowments' [25]. Further, it have been confirmed that intra-industry trade (IIT) had an important role in international tourism as the main pattern of international exchange in tourism services but 'largely independent of the level of development' [25].

By studying bilateral intra-tourism trade for a sample of 14 member states of the European Union during the period 2000–2004, Nowak et al. [26] stated that in contrary to the common view, there was not one-way tourism flows from countries specialized in primary goods, industrial goods and non-tourism services to countries highly specialized in tourism, but there was a high proportion of two-way tourism trade flows with the additional observation that intra-industry trade in tourism services seems to be much higher than in goods trade. Also, the fact that 'trade in vertically differentiated tourism products strongly dominates intra-tourism trade' [26] which means that tourism product quality plays a significant role in intra-European tourism trade was revealed, and that is confirmed by another study finding that there was no 'substantially different patterns between Northern and Southern European countries' [26].

Rising the question about the level of tourism specialization in specific region and economic impact, it was revealed that 'the industries in a region heavily specialized in tourism such as the Balearic Islands have overall higher linkage effects than those on the rest of the country when all national transactions are taken into account' [27].

Looking for empirical relationship between tourist arrivals and trade variables for small island regions, such as Cyprus, it was observed that 'growth in real income stimulates growth in international trade (both exports and imports) and international tourist arrivals to the island. Furthermore, growth in international trade (both exports and imports) also stimulates an increase in international tourist arrivals' [28].

In another similar research concerning the small island destinations, Santana-Gallego et al. [29] found the long-term positive relationship and complementary flows between tourism and trade which means that an increase in the number of arrivals at the same time increases the flow of goods and vice versa.

Vietze in his research claims that 'strict, robust, positive impact of all economic factors like GDP per capita and the openness to trade on tourism expenditures per capita' was found [30], but the influence of other factors (literacy rate, attractiveness of domestic tourism) was rather weak.

Focusing on the effect that German tourism to Spain has on German imports of Spanish wine in context of international trade and tourism [31], it was observed that 'export- (and thus economy-) promoting effects on international tourism, in some cases at least, are statistically significant, positive, relatively long-lasting and considerable in magnitude' [31].

With regard to tourism industry, the role of People's Republic of China (PRC) became increasingly influential in the last decade; apart from becoming one of world's most popular destinations (fourth in arrivals in 2014), it is also the world's top tourism source market with growing expenditure abroad [4], in [32]. If the number of outbound Chinese tourists in 2008 was just over 20 millions, this number increased to 133 in 2015 [33], in [32]. There has also been exceptional increase in how many Chinese tourists spend abroad—in 2014 they've spent a record USD 164.9 billion [4], in [32]. These data point to several important processes within PRC as well as globally: the growing middle classes in China and the complex relationship between modernity and consumption, the emergence of tourism as one of the leading economic sectors in the world, the effects of economic crisis on the global economic restructuring, etc. [32].

There are a few important facts about the actual state in Chinese outbound tourism flows [34]:

- Continued expanding and maintaining a high growth rate of outbound market.
- Spatial imbalance of outbound market. Eastern area is in 'or close to the threshold interval of an explosive phase' [34]; in central and western area, outbound tourism just has become common.
- Almost 70% outbound tourist flows are directed to short-haul destinations (Hong Kong, Macao and Taiwan), showing transitional characteristics connecting domestic and international tourism, travel purpose, stay duration and consumption per capita.
- China's outbound market, in relative sense according to its large population, is far beyond developed countries.
- Consumer behaviour of Chinese outbound tourists is more inspired by shopping than enjoying the cultural activities in destination.
- China's outbound tourism is 'still in a preliminary stage of development' [34].

Shan and Wilson found by researching relationship between international tourism and trade regarding Chinese outbound tourism 'a two-way Granger causality between international travel and international trade and hence imply that trade flows do link with tourism in the case of China' [35].

There are a few aspects in relationship among international tourism flows and economic effects in case of China, which were stressed in recent research [36].

Bilateral international tourism flows were positively related with economic size and negatively with distance between origin and destination countries, regarding China.

Common land border, language and religion strongly influence in increasing the number of inbound arrivals in China.

Developing bilateral trade promotes international tourism flows in both directions.

Some studies point to empirical figures in relation to foreign-exchange earnings from Chinese outbound tourism and main factors of economic growth.

In research study regarding tourism flows from Mainland China in Taiwan, the increase of foreign-exchange earnings from tourism to gross domestic product (GDP) ratio from 1.48% in 2008 to 2.45% in 2012, with USD 1610 real average consumption per tourist [37] has been noted. It is also stated that 'macroeconomic factors (e.g. GDP) have significant effects on foreign-exchange earnings from tourism as expected' [37].

The scope and structure of Chinese outbound tourism flows regarding the international trade, particularly in Slovenia and Montenegro, will be presented in one of the following chapters.

3. Research hypotheses and methodology

According to the literature review, we propose four hypotheses:

- H1: Export in China and the number of overnights of Chinese tourists both in Slovenia and Montenegro are in strong and positive correlation.
- H2: Expenditure of Chinese tourists visiting Slovenia and Montenegro increases every year.
- H3: Share of expenditure of Chinese tourists visiting Slovenia and Montenegro in the export in China increases every year.
- H4: Share of expenditure of Chinese tourists and export in China in national GDP increases every year.

For the purpose of this scientific research, the study mostly based on secondary data was conducted. The aims of this text were to analyze the relevant statistical data about Chinese outbound tourists and their consumption in tourism, in the light of trading and export carried both directly and indirectly through tourism, and to analyze how these variables influence economies of Slovenia and Montenegro. The Pearson's correlation to determine the intensity and direction of influence among variables in the H1 was used.

The statistical data related to China, Slovenia and Montenegro were collected from the SURS [38] and Statistical Office of Montenegro (MONSTAT) [39] but from UNWTO [4], WTTC [40] and other relevant organizations' reports as well.

Current prices were used for GDP, export trade and tourist expenditure calculations.

Processing of statistical data available on the statistical offices of these three countries was considered in the context of the global contemporary trends.

4. Results

In the following part of the text, the most important findings of the study are presented.

4.1. China

4.1.1. China trade market

According to The Observatory of Economic Complexity [41], China is the largest export economy in the world and the 37th most complex economy according to the economic complexity index (ECI). In 2014, China exported \$2.37T and imported \$1.53T, resulting in a positive trade balance of \$834B. In 2014 the GDP of China was \$10.4T and its GDP per capita was \$13.2k.

The top exports of China are computers ($208B), broadcasting equipment ($157B), telephones ($107B), integrated circuits ($61.5B) and office machine parts ($46.9B), using the 1992 revision of the harmonized system (HS) classification. The top export destinations of China are the United States ($432B), Hong Kong ($258B), Japan ($166B), Germany ($101B) and South Korea ($88.9B).

Its top imports are crude petroleum ($205B), integrated circuits ($135B), iron ore ($73.4B), gold ($63.9B) and cars ($55.2B). The top import origins are South Korea ($142B), the United States ($134B), other Asian countries ($131B), Japan ($131B) and Germany ($96.7B).[1]

4.1.2. *China outbound tourism*

The number of Chinese outbound tourists started to increase substantially in 2010 and almost doubled in just 3 years [42], in [43].

As it has been already mentioned in the literature review, nowadays China became the world's top tourism source market and at the same time one of most visited tourist destinations in the world [4], in [32].

Some of the most popular countries among Chinese tourists are Japan, South Korea, Taiwan and Hong Kong, followed by France, Italy and Switzerland (sixth, seventh and eighth in 2015) and Germany (tenth in 2015) [44], in [43].

Apart from the significant increase of the number of outbound Chinese tourists [33], in [32], exceptional increase in Chinese tourists expenditure is also determined [4], in [32].

When it is about the countries of Central and Southeastern Europe, they actually are not in the forefront of Chinese tourists' visits. Despite this, some countries have experienced a fast growth in this sector; Greece reported the highest growth among European countries (160% in 2014), while Romania, Bulgaria and Serbia also showed considerable increase of Chinese visits. An important aspect of this growth is the forming of regional clusters that have a spillover effect for countries that are part of these clusters [33], in [43].

4.2. Slovenia

4.2.1. *Slovenia trade market*

According to report of The Observatory of Economic Complexity about Slovenia [45], it is stated that Slovenia is the 64th largest export economy in the world and the 12th most complex economy according to the economic complexity index (ECI). In 2014, Slovenia exported $30.7B and imported $30.2B, resulting in a positive trade balance of $438M. In 2014 the GDP of Slovenia was $49.5B and its GDP per capita was $30.4k.

External trade of Slovenia for the period 2005–2015 is presented in **Figure 1**.

---

[1] For the purpose of this analysis, we used different bases, and the original curency is kept. Namely, USD was used from international basis, while EUR was used from the national statistical offices of Slovenia and Montenegro.

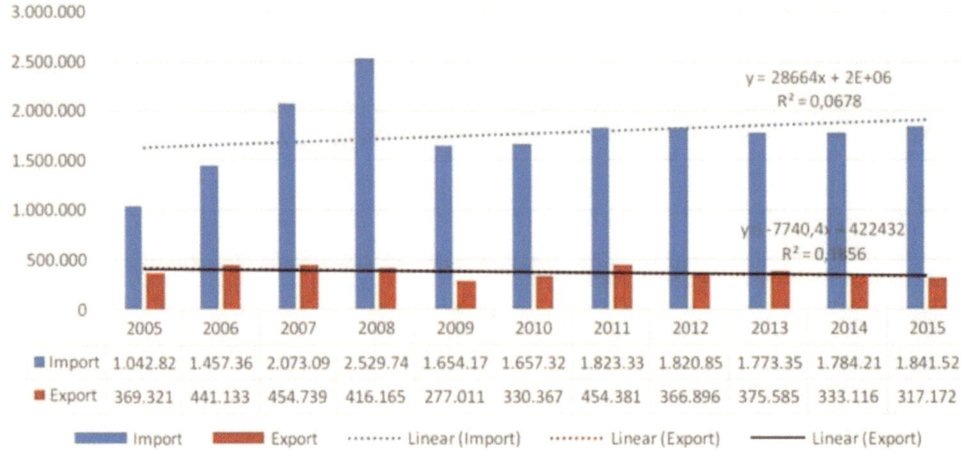

Figure 1. External trade of Slovenia, 2005–2015 (000, Eur). Source: 'Statistični urad Republike Slovenije (SURS)', Ljubljana, 2016.

The top exports of Slovenia are cars ($2.81B), packaged medicaments ($2.64B), refined petroleum ($1.16B), vehicle parts ($947M) and electrical lighting and signalling equipment ($481M), using the 1992 revision of the harmonized system (HS) classification. The top export destinations of Slovenia are Germany ($6.14B), Italy ($3.52B), Austria ($2.54B), Croatia ($2.12B) and France ($1.6B).

Structure of external trade—export of Slovenia in the period 2005–2015 is presented in **Table 1**.

Its top imports are refined petroleum ($2.37B), cars ($1.87B), packaged medicaments ($959M), vehicle parts ($732M) and petroleum gas ($476M). The top import origins are Germany ($5.01B), Italy ($4.56B), Austria ($2.67B), China ($1.75B) and Croatia ($1.28B) [46].

The development of Slovenian export and import in China since 2005 until 2015 is shown in **Table 2**.

4.2.2. Inbound tourism in Slovenia

4.2.2.1. Tourist arrivals and overnights

Regarding the data from economic accounts for tourism, Slovenia [46], the arrival of foreign tourists to Slovenia has been growing steadily since 2005 (**Table 3**). In 2015, 2.6 million arrivals and 6.3 million overnight stays were recorded, exceeding the threshold of 6 million for the first time [38]. The key markets are still represented by countries within Europe, especially in the region (Italy, Austria, Germany, The Russian Federation, The Netherlands, Croatia, the United Kingdom, Serbia and Hungary) [38]. The average length of foreign tourists' overnight stay, already rather short in 2005 (2.83 nights), was further shortened in 2015 (2.43 nights) [43]. Overall, tourism industries contributed 13% to the Slovenian GDP and employed 13% of the active labour force in Slovenia [38].

http://dx.doi.org/10.5772/66628

	Food and drink	Industrial materials	Fuels and lubricants	Capital goods (except transport means), their parts and accessories	Transport vehicles and their parts and accessories	Consumer goods, not elsewhere specified	Products, not elsewhere specified
2005	381,048	5,098,218	307,112	2,539,690	2,842,560	3,222,426	6000
2006	427,745	6,161,413	464,584	3,167,269	3,151,741	3,619,169	12,131
2007	488,232	6,801,647	387,956	3,697,548	4,105,952	4,131,784	15,935
2008	636,571	6,732,563	606,331	4,061,561	3,905,568	4,075,417	24,059
2009	538,261	5,028,804	540,507	3,082,998	3,355,559	3,711,078	12,133
2010	663,081	6,054,759	811,052	3,442,234	3,663,220	3,992,573	12,425
2011	744,523	6,934,760	1,224,344	3,843,085	3,896,654	4,336,415	19,514
2012	707,635	6,949,252	1,383,825	3,943,856	3,666,207	4,388,555	21,354
2013	755,117	7,071,464	1,458,825	4,063,910	3,638,918	4,541,258	19,212
2014	814,562	7,472,399	1,443,869	4,250,636	4,130,310	4,801,361	22,513
2015	873,172	7,794,159	1,297,650	4,427,189	4,644,576	4,876,346	26,927
Growth index 2015/ 2005	2.29	1.53	4.23	1.74	1.63	1.51	4.49

Source: 'Statistični urad Republike Slovenije (SURS)', Ljubljana, 2016.

Table 1. Structure of external trade, export—Slovenia, 2005–2015 (000, Eur).

	Export			Import		
	Total	**China**	**China in total export %**	**Total**	**China**	**China in total import %**
2005	14,397,054	36,248	0.25	15,804,786	196,800	1.25
2006	17,004,052	55,540	0.33	18,354,870	245,976	1.34
2007	19,629,054	66,037	0.34	21,521,340	346,400	1.61
2008	20,042,070	77,689	0.39	23,038,016	441,852	1.92
2009	16,269,340	76,779	0.47	17,275,937	367,302	2.13
2010	18,639,344	102,116	0.55	20,100,589	512,688	2.55
2011	20,999,296	99,051	0.47	22,555,089	575,830	2.55
2012	21,060,685	135,589	0.64	22,077,660	618,202	2.80
2013	21,548,704	126,850	0.59	22,114,150	538,678	2.44
2014	22,935,649	139,405	0.61	22,580,164	621,365	2.75
2015	23,940,020	147,715	0.62	23,304,943	758,526	3.25
Average	19,678,661	96,638	0.48	20,793,413	474,874	2.24

Source: 'Statistični urad Republike Slovenije (SURS)', Ljubljana, 2016.

Table 2. China in the total export and import of Slovenia, 2005–2015 (000 Eur).

		Foreign tourists	Chinese tourists	China's tourists share	Chinese tourists base index 2005	Chinese tourists base share index 2005	Foreign tourist nights	Chinese tourist nights
2005	Arrivals	1,555,000	1754	0.113%	1.00	1.00	2.83	2.20
	Accommodations	4,399,000	3862	0.088%	1.00	1.00		
2006	Arrivals	1,617,000	2615	0.162%	1.49	1.43	2.78	1.86
	Accommodations	4,489,000	4874	0.109%	1.26	1.24		
2007	Arrivals	1,751,332	3503	0.200%	2.00	1.77	2.78	2.43
	Accommodations	4,867,900	8514	0.175%	2.20	1.99		
2008	Arrivals	1,957,691	4887	0.250%	2.79	2.21	2.73	2.06
	Accommodations	5,351,282	10,090	0.189%	2.61	2.15		
2009	Arrivals	1,823,931	5627	0.309%	3.21	2.74	2.71	2.00
	Accommodations	4,936,293	11,230	0.227%	2.91	2.59		
2010	Arrivals	1,869,106	8205	0.439%	4.68	3.89	2.67	1.87
	Accommodations	4,997,031	15,348	0.307%	3.97	3.50		
2011	Arrivals	2,036,652	11,050	0.543%	6.30	4.81	2.68	1.97
	Accommodations	5,463,931	21,785	0.399%	5.64	4.54		
2012	Arrivals	2,120,763	15,208	0.717%	8.67	6.36	2.68	1.54
	Accommodations	5,676,273	23,411	0.412%	6.06	4.70		
2013	Arrivals	2,258,570	19,801	0.877%	11.29	7.77	2.64	1.48
	Accommodations	5,962,251	29,321	0.492%	7.59	5.60		
2014	Arrivals	2,410,824	23,827	0.988%	13.58	8.76	2.53	1.51
	Accommodations	6,090,409	35,915	0.590%	9.30	6.72		
2015	Arrivals	2,620,471	37,234	1.421%	10.63	12.60	2.43	1.44
	Accommodations	6,370,264	53,617	0.842%	6.30	9.59		

Source: 'Statistični urad Republike Slovenije (SURS)', Ljubljana, 2016.
Arrivals of tourists to an accommodation facility are defined as the number of persons arriving to the accommodation facility and checking-in. Arrivals include all persons irrespective of their age (including children whose accommodation is free of charge). Accommodations denote every night which a tourist actually spends at an accommodation facility (overnight or shorter) or if only checked-in (a person's physical presence is not necessary) 'Statistični urad Republike Slovenije (SURS)', Ljubljana, 2016.

Table 3. Number of arrivals and accommodations of foreign tourists in Slovenia between 2005 and 2015[1].

The number of Chinese tourists in Slovenia is on the rise (**Table 3**).

In comparison to 2005, an increase of 10.63 index points in 2015 can be observed. In 2015 the number of Chinese tourists' accommodations was 53,617 representing 0.8% of all foreign tourists' accommodations in Slovenia and 1.4% of all foreign arrivals. Although the percent remains low, it shows a clear positive trend which may predict the increase in the share of all foreign tourists in the near future.

The number of arrivals and accommodations of foreign tourists in Slovenia between 2005 and 2015 is shown in **Table 3**.

The above data also show the average length of Chinese tourists' stay in Slovenia. In 2005 Chinese tourists stayed for 2.20 nights on average, which shortened in the subsequent years down to less than a day and a half (1.44) in 2015. This trend should raise some concern among tourism planners and stakeholders as it may reflect the decrease in the attractiveness of the destination. Although it is true that Chinese tourists prefer tours involving multiple countries, this trend nonetheless points to possible inadequacies regarding the tourism offer for Chinese guests in Slovenia.

4.2.2.2. Tourism consumption in Slovenia

The total tourism expenditure in Slovenia in 2012 was estimated at EUR 3,449 million and in 2014 at EUR 3,515 million and grew by 1.9% in this period. Other components of tourism consumption were estimated at EUR 77 and 73 million, respectively; the total internal tourism consumption was therefore EUR 3,526 million in 2012 and EUR 3,587 million in 2014. Out of the total tourism expenditure, expenditure of foreign visitors represented 68% (EUR 2,343 million) in 2012 and 69% (EUR 2,408 million) in 2014 [46].

4.2.2.3. Tourism expenditure of foreign visitors

Among the total expenditure of foreign visitors (**Table 4**), in both years expenditure of foreign tourists, i.e. visitors with at least one overnight, represented around 42% of total expenditure (EUR 974 million in 2012 and EUR 1,017 million in 2014) and expenditure of same-day visitors (excursionists or transit guests) around 58% (EUR 1,369 million in 2012 and EUR 1,391 million in 2014). Expenditure of foreign tourists grew by 4.4% in this period and expenditure of same-day visitors by 1.6%; the total increase of expenditures of foreign visitors was 2.8%.

Tourist expenditure by foreign visitors in Slovenia for the years of 2012 and 2014 is presented in **Table 4**.

	2012		**2014**	
	Mio EUR	**%**	**Mio EUR**	**%**
Expenditure by foreign tourists	974	42	1017	42
Expenditure by foreign same-day visitors	1369	58	1391	58
Total	2343	100	2408	100

Source: Statistični urad Republike Slovenije (SURS), 'economic accounts for tourism, Slovenia, 2012, estimation for 2014', 2016.

Table 4. Tourism expenditure by foreign visitors, 2012 and 2014.

In Slovenia in 2011 the consumption of Chinese guests reached 2.8 million EUR (daily consumption of food service 80 EUR, the consumption of indirect consumption 50 EUR [47], and regarding to that fact we can expect 2015 220 EUR per day. There is also a casino consumption which in 2011 amounted 8.3 million EUR in 2015.

4.3. Montenegro

4.3.1. Montenegro trade market

In the report of The Observatory of Economic Complexity—Montenegro, it was noted that Montenegro is the 162nd largest export economy in the world. In 2014, Montenegro exported $614M and imported $2.62B, resulting in a negative trade balance of $2B. In 2014 the GDP of Montenegro was $4.59B and its GDP per capita was $15.1k [48].

The development and trend of external trade—export and import since 2005 until 2015—are presented in **Figure 2**.

The import has been increasing with the growth index per year of 108.07, which represent 8.07% of the growth for the period of these 10 years. At the other hand, the export has been increasing with the growth index per year of 100.44, which represent 0.44% of the growth for the period of these 10 years. The trade balance for the period of 2005 to 2015 was 226.33 [49].

The top exports of Montenegro are raw aluminium ($112M), recreational boats ($79.3M), cars ($44.6M), refined petroleum ($39.9M) and dried legumes ($32.2M), using the 1992 revision of the harmonized system (HS) classification. The top export destinations of Montenegro are

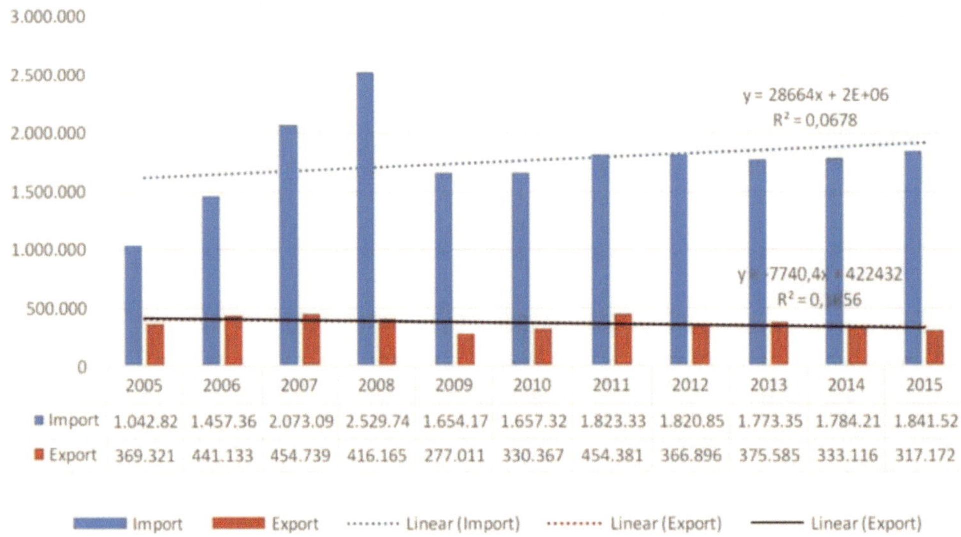

Figure 2. External trade of Montenegro, 2005–2015 (000,Eur). Source: Z. za statistiku C. G. Monstat, 'Spoljnotrgovinski promet Crne Gore 2005–2015', Podgorica, Montenegro, 2016.

Malta ($77.2M), Serbia ($68.1M), Italy ($53M), Greece ($43.3M) and Bosnia and Herzegovina ($42.2M) [48].

Structure of external trade—export of Montenegro in the period 2005–2014 is presented in **Table 5**.

According to the structure of export of Montenegro, in the period from 2005 until 2014, industrial materials, food and drink and other consumer goods had the most important role. The share of other products, capital goods, fuels and lubricants and transport vehicles in the total amount of export was much smaller.

Its top imports are refined petroleum ($241M), pig meat ($98.4M), cars ($98M), packaged medicaments ($57.8M) and raw aluminium ($50M). The top import origins are Serbia ($695M), Greece ($194M), China ($191M), Croatia ($160M) and Italy ($156M) [48].

Share of China in the total export and import of Montenegro in the period 2005–2015 is presented in **Table 6**.

For the observed period from 2005 to 2015, the average share of China in the total export of Montenegro was 0.51%, while at the same time, the average share of China in the total import of Montenegro was 6.03%, which shows that China presents significantly more important partner in import than in export of Montenegro.

	Food and drink	Industrial materials	Fuels and lubricants	Capital goods (except transport means), their parts and accessories	Transport vehicles and their parts and accessories	Consumer goods, not elsewhere specified	Products, not elsewhere specified
2005	177,241	237,548	60,363	129,158	99,312	160,434	178,771
2006	214,755	365,422	201,610	203,231	153,474	234,470	84,398
2007	281,867	524,387	292,725	324,241	257,244	338,742	53,888
2008	384,611	692,362	343,702	391,337	294,875	421,869	985
2009	358,108	432,599	189,823	216,096	128,066	328,424	1054
2010	368,950	443,956	189,060	207,303	119,421	326,008	2630
2011	400,178	462,930	305,076	189,059	118,619	338,652	8823
2012	405,301	428,698	315,438	183,583	143,873	342,830	1128
2013	416,696	419,413	248,602	187,573	145,783	350,594	4691
2014	444,905	421,798	226,751	206,267	117,264	356,377	1107
Index 2014/ 2005	2.51	1.78	3.76	1.60	1.18	2.22	0.01

Source: Z. za statistiku C. G. Monstat, 'Spoljnotrgovinski promet Crne Gore 2005–2015', Podgorica, Montenegro, 2016.

Table 5. Structure of external trade, export—Montenegro, 2005–2014 (000, Eur).

	Export			Import		
	Total	**China**	**China in total export %**	**Total**	**China**	**China in total import %**
2005	369,321	0	0.00	1,042,828	33,326	3.20
2006	441,133	0	0.00	1,457,361	56,874	3.90
2007	454,739	62	0.01	2,073,093	100,464	4.85
2008	416,165	152	0.04	2,529,741	123,834	4.90
2009	277,011	95	0.03	1,654,170	90,343	5.46
2010	330,367	149	0.05	1,657,329	88,864	5.36
2011	454,381	748	0.16	1,823,337	103,080	5.65
2012	366,896	3802	1.04	1,820,850	130,615	7.17
2013	375,585	3907	1.04	1,773,352	142,895	8.06
2014	333,116	2561	0.77	1,784,214	132,736	7.44
2015	317,172	7904	2.49	1,841,524	189,591	10.30
Average	375,990	1762	0.51	1,768,891	108,420	6.03

Source: Z. za statistiku C. G. Monstat, 'Spoljnotrgovinski promet Crne Gore 2005–2015', Podgorica, Montenegro, 2016.

Table 6. China in total export and import of Montenegro, 2005–2015 (000 Eur).

4.3.2. Inbound tourism in Montenegro

4.3.2.1. Tourist arrivals and overnights

The Statistical Office of Montenegro (MONSTAT) has been collating information on Chinese tourists since 2014. The data on the years prior to 2014 are not available (the information on Chinese tourists were collated under the category 'Other'). Therefore, the direct comparison with Slovenia is only possible for the last 2 years.

The total number of Chinese tourists' arrivals (**Table 7**) in 2014 was 7,932, which represents 0.59% of the total foreign tourists' arrivals. Looking at the overnight stays, Chinese tourists realized 14,432 overnight stays or 0.17% of the total foreign tourist overnight stays in Montenegro. The average length of stay was 1.82 days, far below the total foreign tourists' stay of 6.36 days in 2014. Based on these data, Montenegro is still heavily characterized by the coastal tourism of long summer vacations. In this regard, Chinese are not the 'typical guests' since they spend only a day and a half in Montenegro [50].

In 2015, foreign tourists in Montenegro realized a total of 1,559,924 arrivals and 10,307,371 accommodations. In the same year, the number of Chinese tourists compared to the year before increased to 13,362 arrivals and 18,170 accommodations. While these numbers still represent a marginal share among all foreign tourists, the segment of Chinese tourists shows a minor increase (0.80% of total foreign arrivals and 0.16% of overnight stays). What may be seen as potentially worrying is the substantial decrease in the average length of stay. Namely, in the year 2015, the length of stay was only 1.35 days, while the total foreign tourists' average length of stay even slightly increased (6.67 days) [43].

Chinese tourists' arrivals and accommodations in Montenegro in the period 2014–2015 are presented in **Table 7**.

		Foreign tourist	Chinese tourists	Chinese tourists' share	Chinese tourists base index 2014	Chinese tourists base share index 2014	Foreign tourists' nights	Chinese tourists' nights
2010	Arrivals	1,087,794					6.41	
	Accommodations	6,977,860						
2011	Arrivals	1,201,099					6.51	
	Accommodations	7,818,803						
2012	Arrivals	1,264,163					6.44	
	Accommodations	8,143,007						
2013	Arrivals	1,324,403					6.35	
	Accommodations	8,414,215						
2014	Arrivals	1,350,297	7932	0.59%			6.37	1.82
	Accommodations	8,596,656	14,432	0.17%				
2015	Arrivals	1,559,924	13,362	0.86%	1.68	1.46	6.61	1.36
	Accommodations	10,307,371	18,170	0.18%	1.26	1.05		

Source: Z. za statistiku C. G. Monstat, 'Dolasci i noćenja turista 2014. godina', 2015.

Table 7. Chinese tourists' arrivals and accommodations in Montenegro, 2014 and 2015.

4.3.2.2. Tourist expenditure

The results of Guest Survey in Montenegro—2010 [51] (**Table 8**) show that the average expenditure for tourist package in Montenegro amounted 528.7 EUR or the price of tourist package per person per overnight was 68.5 EUR. According to more recent Guest Survey conducted by the NTO of Montenegro for 2014 [52], similar findings are determined. The total average cost of travel per person in Montenegro during the summer 2014 amounted to 539.73 EUR, while per person, per day, these costs amounted to 61.92 EUR. Average tourist expenditure in Montenegro in the years of 2010 and 2014 is presented in **Table 8**.

Analyzing the tourist expenditure according to the type of accommodation, in 2010 the average price for tourist package per person per day in hotels amounted 84.5 EUR, which is twice as much in comparison with private accommodation/apartments/rooms (43.1 EUR) [51]. In 2014, the highest average tourist expenditure was among hotel guests as well, a total of 86.72 EUR per person per day, while the guests in resorts tend to spend significantly less, but comparing to those tourists staying in private accommodation, they actually spent more for their tourist packages [52].

EUR	2010	2014
Tourist package per person	528.70	539.73
Tourist package per person per day	68.50	61.92

Source: Nacionalna turistička organizacija Crne Gore, 'Guest Survey (2014) Stavovi i potrošnja turista u Crnoj Gori', Podgorica, Montenegro, 2014.

Table 8. Average tourist expenditure in Montenegro in 2010 and 2014.

When it comes to the country origin of the tourists, in 2010 the average amount for tourist package per person was the cheapest for tourists who came from the region (360.6 EUR). On the other side, tourists from EU countries and other countries paid their packages by doubled prices (611.0 EUR and 713.8 EUR) for tourist package in Montenegro. At the other side, during the summer 2014, the highest average expenditure per trip (per person in EUR) was realized by Russian tourists (855.51 EUR), followed by tourists from Ukraine and Belarus (795.37 EUR), Scandinavia (713.63 EUR), the United Kingdom (657.23 EUR), France (642.49 EUR), Germany (567 EUR), Italy (527 EUR), Poland, The Czech Republic and Hungary (456 EUR), Kosovo, Macedonia, Albania and Romania (452 EUR), Bosnia and Herzegovina and Croatia (361.02 EUR) and Serbia (313.13 EUR).

5. Discussion

Based on both the literature review and analysis of statistical data (**Tables 10** and **11**), it could be concluded that the H1 is proved.

Namely, a strong and positive correlation between export in China and the number of overnights of Chinese tourists in Slovenia (r = .946), which is also proved in another research [36], is identified, but when it comes to the relation of share of export of China in total export and share of overnights of China in total overnights, the correlation is not so strong (r = .891). In case of Montenegro, we can assume that H1 is partially proved due to lack of time series data.

Similar findings are determined in the study conducted in Cyprus, which showed that growth in both exports and imports stimulates an increase in international tourist arrivals [28]. In addition, in one study concerning the small island destinations, an increase in the number of arrivals at the same time increasing the flow of goods and vice versa is concluded [29].

Positive impact of all economic factors, including trade, on tourism expenditures per capita is also identified in Vietze's study [30], while the fact that export-promoting effects on international tourism are statistically significant and positive is also found in the research concerning the effect that German tourism to Spain has on German imports of Spanish wine [31].

When it is about H2, we can also state that this hypothesis for both countries is proved, since the expenditure of Chinese tourists visiting Slovenia and Montenegro in the observed period increases every year (**Tables 3**, **7**, **10** and **11**).

		2005	2010	2012	2014	2015
World	Total consumption —EUR	551,201,753,209	697,985,300,603	837,681,032,402	968,079,895,111	1,106,344,867,836
	Cross border	797,000,000	939,000,000	1,035,000,000	1,133,000,000	1,184,000,000
	The average spending per trip—EUR	692	743	809	854	934
China	Total outbound tourism consumption—EUR	17,670,879,735	41,203,648,390	79,482,293,307	123,271,331,818	205,643,648,323
	Cross border	31,000,000	57,400,000	83,200,000	116,000,000	133,000,000
	The average spending per trip—EUR	570	718	955	1,063	1,546
Indicators	Share of consumption: China in total	3.21%	5.90%	9.49%	12.73%	18.59%
	Share of cross border: China in total	3.89%	6.11%	8.04%	10.24%	11.23%
	Share of average spending per trip: China in total	82%	97%	118%	124%	165%

Table 9. General analysis of tourist expenditure: world-China (2005–2015).

		2005	2010	2012	2014	2015
Slovenia	GDP	29,227,000,000	36,252,000,000	35,988,000,000	37,303,000,000	38,543,000,000
	Total—export	14,397,054,000	18,639,344,000	21,060,685,000	22,935,649,000	23,940,020,000
	China—export	36,248,000	102,116,000	135,589,000	139,405,000	147,715,000
	Share of export: China in total	0.25%	0.55%	0.64%	0.61%	0.62%
	Share of total export in GDP	49.26%	51.42%	58.52%	61.48%	62.11%
	Share of export: China in GDP	0.12%	0.28%	0.38%	0.37%	0.38%
	Total—overnights	4,399,000	4,997,031	5,676,273	6,090,409	6,370,264
	China—overnights	3,862	15,348	23,411	35,231	41,141
	Share of overnights: China in total	0.09%	0.31%	0.41%	0.58%	0.65%
	Total—expenditure by foreign tourists per day			172	167	

	2005	2010	2012	2014	2015
China—expenditure by foreign tourists per day	80	120	202	208	220
Share of expenditure by foreign tourists per day: China in total			118%	124%	
China—total expenditure by foreign tourists per day	308,960	1,841,760	4,740,211	7,318,462	9,051,020
Share: China—expenditure by foreign tourists per day in export to China	0.85%	1.80%	3.50%	5.25%	6.13%
China—foreign same-day visitors			3,348	3,314	11,444
China—expenditure by foreign same-day visitors		55	65	75	80
China—total expenditure by foreign same-day visitors			217,620	248,550	915,520
Tourism expenditure by foreign visitors	1,459,063,464	1,951,356,754	2,088,358,295	2,242,656,128	2,334,818,715
Tourism expenditure by Chinese visitors	308,960	1,841,760	4,957,831	7,567,012	9,966,540
Share of expenditure by Chinese visitors in expenditure by foreign visitors	0.02%	0.09%	0.24%	0.34%	0.43%
Share tourism expenditure by foreign visitors in total exports	10.13%	10.47%	9.92%	9.78%	9.75%
Share of expenditure by foreign visitors in GDP	4.99%	5.38%	5.80%	6.01%	6.06%
Share of expenditure by Chinese visitors in expenditure in GDP	0.00%	0.01%	0.01%	0.02%	0.03%
Gambling		5,050,000	9,900,000	14,430,000	17,395,000
Total China—expenditure	308,960	6,891,760	14,857,831	21,997,012	27,361,540
Share: total China—expenditure in export to China	0.85%	6.75%	10.96%	15.78%	18.52%
Share of total China expenditure by Chinese visitors in total export	0.00%	0.04%	0.07%	0.10%	0.11%
Share of total China expenditure by Chinese visitors in GDP	0.00%	0.02%	0.04%	0.06%	0.07%

Table 10. General analysis of GDP, export trade and tourist expenditure in Slovenia (2005–2015).

http://dx.doi.org/10.5772/66628

		2005	2010	2012	2014	2015
Montenegro	GDP	1,815,000,000	3,125,090,000	3,181,477,000	3,457,922,000	3,993,000,000
	Total—export	369,321,000	330,367,000	366,896,000	333,116,000	317,172,000
	China—export		149,133	3,801,660	2,561,000	7,904,000
	Share of export: China in total		0.0%	1.0%	0.8%	2.5%
	Share of total export in GDP	20.35%	10.57%	11.53%	9.63%	7.94%
	Share of export: China in GDP		0.005%	0.119%	0.074%	0.198%
	Total—overnights	4,900,000	6,977,860	8,143,007	8,596,656	10,307,371
	China—overnights				14,432	18,170
	Share of overnights: China in total				0.17%	0.18%
	Total—expenditure by foreign tourists per day		68.50		61.92	
	China—expenditure by foreign tourists per day				180	200
	Share of expenditure by foreign tourists per day: China in total				291%	
	China—total expenditure by foreign tourists per day				2,597,760	3,634,000
	Share: China—expenditure by foreign tourists per day in export to China				101.44%	45.98%
	Tourism expenditure by foreign visitors	217,238,338	547,880,935	638,975,299	680,272,359	808,206,478
	Tourism expenditure by Chinese visitors				2,597,760	3,634,000
	Share of expenditure by Chinese visitors in expenditure by foreign visitors				0.38%	0.45%
	Share tourism expenditure by foreign visitors in total exports	58.82%	165.84%	174.16%	204.21%	254.82%
	Share of expenditure by foreign visitors in GDP	11.97%	17.53%	20.08%	19.67%	20.24%
	Share of expenditure by Chinese visitors in expenditure in GDP				0.08%	0.09%
	Total China—expenditure				2,597,760	3,634,000
	Share: total China—expenditure in export to China				101.44%	45.98%
	Share of total China expenditure by Chinese visitors in total export				0.78%	1.15%
	Share of total China expenditure by Chinese visitors in GDP				0.08%	0.09%

Table 11. General analysis of GDP, export trade and tourist expenditure in Montenegro (2005–2015).

Analyzing the expenditure of Chinese tourists visiting Slovenia and Montenegro (**Tables 10** and **11**) and the amount of total export in China (**Tables 2, 6, 10** and **11**), it could be concluded that the share of tourist expenditure in Slovenia in the export in China increases every year, while the results for Montenegro are not available enough. Based on that, we can state that H3 is proved for Slovenia and it is partially proved for Montenegro.

Furthermore, analyzing the expenditure of Chinese tourists visiting Slovenia and Montenegro and export from these two countries into China (**Tables 10** and **11**), we can conclude that the share of both variables in national GDP increases every year. Based on that, we can state that H4 is proved.

6. Conclusion

Analyzing statistical data of China, Slovenia and Montenegro dedicated to GDP, international trade (export and import), but also the number of tourist arrivals and overnights and tourism consumption, based on the consulting of the relevant literature, important conclusions of this study were made.

Tourist expenditure of foreign tourists has very important share in the total amount of export in Slovenia (10.13–9.75%) and even more significant share in Montenegro (58.82–254.82%), especially comparing to world average share of 6% [4]. At the same time, the share of tourist expenditure of Chinese tourists in both countries is below the average (Slovenia 0.04%–0.11%; Montenegro 0.78%–1.15%). Dynamically observed, the significant growth of the share of Chinese tourist expenditure in the total export is determined.

Growth index of 3.09 for Slovenia in the period 2010–2015, and growth index of 1.47 for Montenegro in the period 2014–2015, implies future significant influence of 'invisible export' in China, for both countries.

The share of foreign tourist expenditure in GDP of Slovenia (4.99%–6.06%) is below the world average, while this share in GDP of Montenegro (11.97%–20.24%) is significantly beyond the world average, which is 9% [4]. The share of tourist expenditure of Chinese tourists in GDP of both countries (**Tables 10** and **11**) is very low but with the significantly high growth index of 5.09 for Slovenia during the period of 5 years and of 1.21 for Montenegro during the period of 2 years, which again confirms previous claim.

The Chinese tourist expenditure is over average expenditure (**Tables 9–11**), especially for Montenegro. The total Chinese tourist expenditure in Slovenia, including gambling, is very important with tendency to increase. Yet, the Chinese tourist expenditure is an important part of export in China. China could become a very important partner in the international trade, as an 'invisible export', as well.

The effect of tourist spending at the destination will be proportionate to its economical size [36], which in case of Slovenia and Montenegro means that Chinese tourists will spend less days in one single destination regarding to staying in the West Balkan region (more destinations) which is confirmed in another study [43].

It is necessary that appropriate incentive measurements be established within strategic policies of both Slovenia and Montenegro in order to make more attractive conditions for tourism promotion in China. It would be also of great importance that these two countries provide better conditions related to their tourist products in order to motivate Chinese tourists to stay longer at the destinations and, based on that fact, to ensure that their tourist expenditure could significantly increase. Establishing a creative and innovative tourist product, which would be at the same time adjusted according to the specific characteristics and requirements of Chinese tourists, would be the right way to achieve that goal.

Limitation of this research lies in the fact that the study was conducted only based on open statistical data, not including empirical research. Additionally, due to the currency differences (USD, EUR), some differences in amounts, comparing to general statistical data, could be found. Current prices were used for GDP, export trade and tourist expenditure calculations.

Furthermore, the relation among the economic growth, international trade and tourism flows from China was not examined.

Author details

Andrej Raspor[1,2]*, Ana Stranjančević[3,4], Iva Bulatović[3,4] and Darko Lacmanović[3,4]

*Address all correspondence to: andrej.raspor@ceatm.org

1 DOBA Faculty of Applied Business and Social Studies, Maribor, Slovenia

2 School of Advanced Social Studies, Nova Gorica, Slovenia

3 Montenegro Tourism School, Podgorica, Montenegro

4 Mediterranean University, Montenegro

References

[1] Lacmanović D. Selling hotel product on contemporary tourist market. 1st ed. Bar, Montenegro: Univerzitet Mediteran Fakultet za turizam, hotelijerstvo i trgovinu-Bar; 2006. 292 p.

[2] Antunac I. Tourism and theory of economics. Zagreb: Institut za istraživanje turizma; 1985.

[3] Marković S and Marković Z. Tourism economics. Zagreb: Školska knjiga; 1972.

[4] UNWTO. UNWTO tourism highlights 2015 edition. Madrid: UNWTO World Tourism Organization; 2015.

[5] Unković S, Bakić O, Čačić K, Popesku J. Contemporary tourism flows. Beograd: Univerzitete u Beogradu, Ekonomski fakultet; 1991.

[6] UNWTO. Tourism towards 2030 global overview. Madrid: UNWTO World Tourism Organization; 2011. 49 p.

[7] Kester GCJ. International tourism receipts, expenditure and balance. Tourism Economics [Internet]. 2005; 11(2):275–293. Available from: http://www.indexmundi.com/facts/indicators/ST.INT.RCPT.XP.ZS.

[8] Vu JC, Turner L. The economic structure of world tourism. Tourism Economics. 2009; 15 (1):5–21.

[9] Sahli M, Nowak JJ. Does inbound tourism benefit developing countries? A trade theoretic approach. Journal of Travel Research. 2007; 45(4):426–434.

[10] Kulendran N, Wilson K. Is there a relationship between international trade and international travel?. Applied Economics [Internet]. 2000 [cited 2016 Jul 19]; 32(8):1001–1009. Available from: http://www.tandfonline.com/doi/abs/10.1080/000368400322057.

[11] Ivanov S, Webster C. Measuring the impact of tourism on economic growth. Tourism Economics. 2007; 13(3):379–388.

[12] United Nations Conference on Trade and Development. International trade in tourism-related services: issues and options for developing countries. Geneva; 1998.

[13] Chang SC, Lai FT. Intra-continental and intercontinental service trade in the travel and tourism industry. Tourism Economics. 2011; 17(5):963–982.

[14] Kobašić A, Senečić J. Tourism Marketing. Zagreb: Školska knjiga; 1989.

[15] Ivanov SH, Webster C. Tourism's contribution to economic growth: a global analysis for the first decade of the millennium. Tourism Economics. 2013; 19(3):477–508.

[16] Gričar S, Bojnec Š, Karadžić V, Rakočević S. Comparative analysis of tourism-led growth in Slovenia and Montenegro. Managing Global Transitions. 2015; 14(1):75–92.

[17] Pina IPA, Martínez-García MP. An endogenous growth model of international tourism. Tourism Economics. 2013; 19(3):509–529.

[18] Nowak JJ, Sahli M, Cortés-Jiménez I. Tourism, capital good imports and economic growth: theory and evidence for Spain. Tourism Economics. 2007; 13(4):515–536.

[19] Fayed H, Fletcher J. Report: globalization of economic activity: issues for tourism. Tourism Economics. 2002; 8(2):207–230.

[20] Algieri B. International tourism specialisation of small countries. International Journal of Tourism Research [Internet]. 2006; 8:1–12. Available from: http://dx.doi.org/10.1002/jtr.543.

[21] Gunter U, Smeral E. The decline of tourism income elasticities in a global context. Tourism Economics [Internet]. 2014; 22(3):466–483. Available from: http://teu.sagepub.com/lookup/doi/10.5367/te.2014.0431.

[22] Keum K. International tourism and trade flows: a causality analysis using panel data. Tourism Economics. 2011; 17(5):949–962.

[23] Massidda C, Mattana P. A SVECM analysis of the relationship between international tourism arrivals, GDP and trade in Italy. Journal of Travel Research [Internet]. 2013; 52 (1):93–105. Available from: http://jtr.sagepub.com/cgi/doi/10.1177/0047287512457262.

[24] Hong W, Tsui K, Ka M, Fung Y. Causality between business travel and trade volumes: empirical evidence from Hong Kong. Tourism Management. 2016; 52:395–404.

[25] Webster A, Fletcher J, Hardwick P, Morakabati Y. Tourism and empirical applications of international trade theory: a multi-country analysis. Tourism Economics. 2007; 13(4):657–674.

[26] Nowak JJ, Petit S, Sahli M. Intra-tourism trade in Europe. Tourism Economics. 2012; 18 (6):1287–1311.

[27] Soulie J, Valle E. Trade effects of specialization in tourism: an inter-regional input-output model of the Balearic Islands. Tourism Economics. 2014; 20(5):961–985.

[28] Katircioglu S. Tourism, trade and growth: the case of Cyprus. Applied Economics [Internet]. 2009; 41(21):2741–2750. Available from: http://ezproxy.canberra.edu.au/login?url=http://search.ebscohost.com/login.aspx?direct=true&db=bth&AN=43880987.

[29] Santana-Gallego M, Ledesma-Rodríguez F, Pérez-Rodríguez VJ. Tourism and trade in small island regions: the case of the canary islands. Tourism Economics. 2011; 17(1):107–125.

[30] Vietze C. What's pushing international tourism expenditures?. Tourism Economics. 2011; 17(2):237–260.

[31] Fischer C, Gil-Alana LA. The nature of the relationship between international tourism and international trade: the case of German imports of Spanish wine. Applied Economics [Internet]. 2009; 41(11):1345–1359. Available from: http://www.tandfonline.com/doi/abs/10.1080/00036840601019349.

[32] Bofulin M, Raspor A, Stranjančević A, Bulatović I, Lacmanović D. Small destinations in large tourism market: the analysis of western Balkan countries and the Chinese outbound tourism. In: The VIII International Scientific Conference "The role and effectiveness of investments in the integration process of the Balkan societies after Stabilisation Association Agreement". Ulcinj: Institut for scientific research and development; 2016. pp. 130–143.

[33] Arlt WG. Presentation of the results of China-focused tourism route development in Q1 2016. China information day conference China outbound tourism. Budapest, March 3, 2016.

[34] Dai B, Jiang Y, Yang L, Ma Y. China's outbound tourism—stages, policies and choices. Tourism Management. Article in press. 2016. pp. 1–6.

[35] Shan J, Wilson K. Causality between trade and tourism: empirical evidence from China. Applied Economics Letters. 2001; 8(4):279–283.

[36] Wang H, Xi J. The determinant of inbound tourism in China. International Journal of Business and Management [Internet]. 2016 [cited 2016 Jul 19]; 11(2):205–211. Available from: http://search.proquest.com/openview/924cba7f9d65e3dc577be4ce5cd47b3c/1?pq-origsite=gscholar&cbl=307069.

[37] Lee Y, Chang WS. Research note: analysing the effects of economic factors on modelling the diffusion of foreign exchange earnings from tourism in Taiwan. Tourism Economics [Internet]. 2016; I-6. Available from: http://teu.sagepub.com/lookup/doi/10.5367/te.2015.0466.

[38] Republic of Slovenia Statistical Office SURS. Republic of Slovenia Statistical Office SURS, SURS [Internet]. Ljubljana; 2016. Available from: http://www.stat.si/statweb.

[39] Statistical office of Montenegro Monstat. Statistical Yearbook of Montenegro 2015. Podgorica, Montenegro; 2015.

[40] WTTC. Travel & tourism economic impact 2015 Montenegro. London; 2015.

[41] The Observatory of Economic Complexity—OEC. The observatory of economic complexity—China [Internet].. 2016. Available from: http:/atlas.media.mit.edu/en/profile/country/chn/.

[42] Huang S, Keating BW, Kriz A, Heung V. Chinese outbound tourism: an epilogue. Journal of Travel & Tourism Marketing [Internet]. 2015; 32(1–2):153–159. Available from: http://www.tandfonline.com/doi/abs/10.1080/10548408.2014.986018?src=recsys#.VUdC_flVgSU.

[43] Raspor A, Lacmanović D, Stranjančević A, Bulatović I. Chinese tourists in Slovenia and Montenegro: preferences, characteristics and trip motivation. 1st ed.. London: Vega Press LTD; 2016. 101 p.

[44] China National Tourism Administration. Travel China guide: China outbound tourism in 2015 [Internet]. Bejing; 2016. Available from: http://www.travelchinaguide.com/tourism/2015statistics.

[45] The Observatory of Economic Complexity—OEC. The observatory of economic complexity—Slovenia [Internet]. 2016. Available from: http://atlas.media.mit.edu/en/profile/country/svn/.

[46] Economic accounts for tourism, Slovenia, 2012, estimation for 2014 [Internet]. 2016. Available from: http://www.stat.si/StatWeb/en/show-news?id=5678&idp=24&headerbar=19.

[47] Raspor A, Kobal T, Rodic B. Chinese tourists—are they an opportunity for the Slovene and Croatian tourist industry?. Tourism and Hospitality Management [Internet]. 2012; 18 (1):111–125. Available from: http://search.proquest.com/docview/1026947656/13ADE8ADE773CDC1B1C/316?accountid=27540.

[48] The Observatory of Economic Complexity—OEC. The observatory of economic complexity—Montenegro [Internet]. 2016. Available from: http://atlas.media.mit.edu/en/profile/country/mne/.

[49] Statistical office of Montenegro Monstat. External trade of Montenegro 2005–2015 [Internet]. Podgorica, Montenegro; 2016. Available from: http://www.monstat.org/cg/page.php?id=171&pageid=171.

[50] Statistical office of Montenegro Monstat. Arrivals and overnight stays in Montenegro 2010–2015 [Internet]. Podgorica, Montenegro; 2016. Available from: http://www.monstat.org/cg/page.php?id=1378&pageid=44.

[51] National Tourism Organization of Montenegro. Montenegro Guest Survey 2010. Podgorica, Montenegro; 2010.

[52] Nacionalna turistička organizacija Crne Gore. Montenegro Guest survey 2014. Podgorica, Montenegro; 2014.